First published by Busybird Publishing 2024

Copyright © 2024 Ida Di Pastena

ISBN:
Paperback: 978-1-923216-18-1
Ebook: 978-1-923216-19-8

This book is copyright. Apart from any fair dealing for the purposes of study, research, criticism, review, or as otherwise permitted under the Copyright Act, no part may be reproduced by any process without written permission. Enquiries should be made through the publisher.

Cover image: Busybird Publishing

Cover design: Busybird Publishing

Layout and typesetting: Busybird Publishing

Busybird Publishing
2/118 Para Road
Montmorency, Victoria
Australia 3094
www.busybird.com.au

An Interrupted Life

Ida Di Pastena

Some names and identifying characteristics have been changed to protect the privacy of the individuals involved.

For Jev

When we are stricken and cannot bear our lives any longer, then a tree has something to say to us: Be still! Be still! Look at me! Life is not easy, life is not difficult. Those are childish thoughts . . .
Home is neither here nor there. Home is within you, or home is nowhere at all.

Hermann Hesse

Spiritual Healing Trail

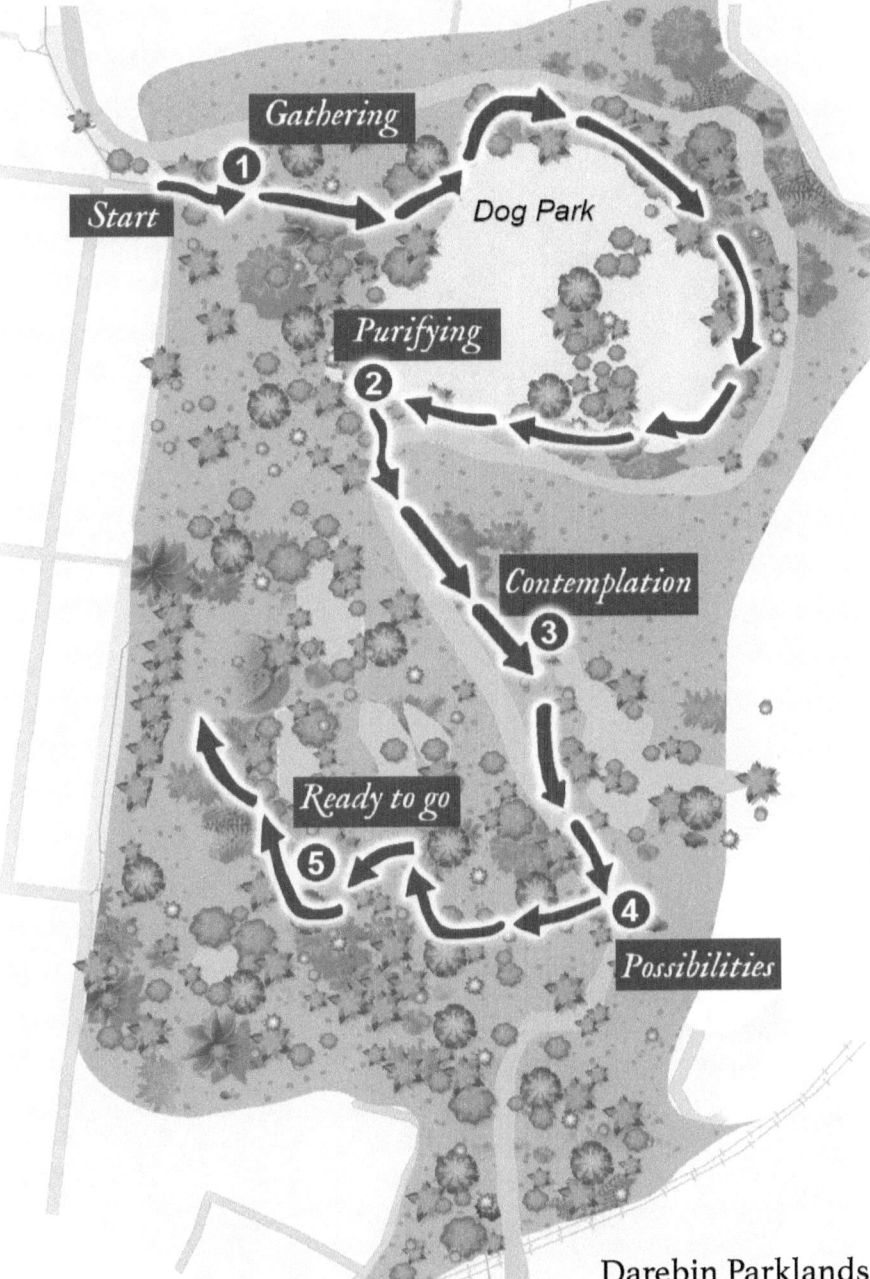

Darebin Parklands

Prologue

It was almost two years into the relationship when things took a different turn; our life together as we knew it was going to change, and in a way neither of us could ever have imagined. Ever.

Yes, the possibility had been there from the start, but it was just that – a *possibility*. Something in the distant future, a shapeless *perhaps*, and it wasn't really going to happen, not really. But happen, it did.

When I told people what had happened, there was a moment of stunned silence, a look of disbelief. They all reacted in different ways, but the enormity of the situation registered with all of them, and the suddenness. I spoke to my doctor about it first, a woman who was always positive and reassuring in her attitude to my obsessive concerns about my health. Before I could finish speaking, she put her face in her hands, shook her head slowly, and repeated, 'Oh, no ... oh, no.' I knew then that what was about to come was beyond my comprehension.

Then I told my friends. One immediately placed her hands on my shoulders, looked at me intently, and said, 'Ida, you didn't sign up for this.' Another said, 'This is huge, but you can do it. And remember, I'll be there for you – all the way.' Another, who lived by Buddhist principles, simply said, 'Think of it as both a challenge and an opportunity. Embrace it.' One of my more matter-of-fact friends asked, 'Do you love him?' And then this from a life-long friend, 'You should walk now.'

But I didn't.

I stayed.

Chapter 1

I've read that after deciding to leave a marriage, particularly a long-standing one, there can be post-divorce doubt and anxiety; a divorce hangover. It's not just about the stress of dividing assets and moving house, it's about the sudden shift in trajectory – once a couple pursuing a shared life, now a single person alone on an unknown path. It's a period of loss and transition as each person struggles to connect with a new identity, no matter who initiated the separation.

Somehow, I think I managed to avoid that when I went through my divorce. Looking back, I have to acknowledge that leaving my twenty-seven-year marriage was one of the easiest decisions I've ever made. And the process of selling, packing, and moving house seemed almost effortless. The family home was sold one weekend, and I bought my new home the very next one. As the real estate agent who was dealing with the sale of our home said, 'Look at that – you sell and buy in a matter of days. So easy. The universe is looking out for you.'

And that's exactly how it felt. I was buoyed by an energy and a sense of calm that I can remember experiencing just once before, at my father's deathbed. He had died an hour prior to the time I walked into his hospital room, but I was immediately enveloped by a warm, soothing energy. It was like an embrace, and the feeling stayed with me for days; so too when I left my marriage.

It wasn't that I felt no sadness. I was sorry, for the pain I caused and the change I thrust upon my husband. But my life needed to change, and I grabbed on with both hands to a force that was propelling me forward. Even now I still find myself looking back with a sense of amazement that it all went so smoothly.

When I told my neighbours, people I had known for years, that the reason we had suited men and women coming to the house regularly was that I was leaving my marriage and that the house was going to be sold, I remember the look of surprise on some of the women's faces. But there weren't questions about why and how, there was just a quiet understanding; an understanding that only older women could know. And it was only much later that I realised I was doing something that might be considered brave. I was *leaving*. I would be facing the unknown at a later age. It wasn't just the inconvenience; it was the loss of security, as well.

There were a few people who responded with condolences, 'I'm sorry to hear that.' It wasn't what I needed to hear, but I understood their feeling that the end of a marriage, particularly a long marriage, can be a sad thing. But I was also convinced that didn't have to be the case; I didn't want it to be sad for us, I wanted to be able to remain friends, good friends.

But sadly, that wasn't to be. My husband wasn't so thrilled about changing his life at such a late stage, a life he felt he was responsible for creating. Afterwards, on the odd occasion that we spoke, he would have a ready answer to any of life's challenges, 'Oh well, it's out of our control.' If there are lessons to be learned in life, that was his: that we have no control. And in many situations, we do have to relinquish control, and not be diminished by it. In some way I felt a little less responsible for his pain when I thought about that; in some way the divorce freed him too. But it would take him a little longer to realise that.

It was only after I told my beautician that I was more than certain I was doing the right thing. She *congratulated* me. It was as if I had just told her I was getting married instead. It made me smile for days. And it made me feel just a little excited about what was to come.

So, after twenty-seven years of marriage, I found myself living alone without anyone's approbation or disapprobation – as my single friend Heather said I would – and she was right. I didn't have to puzzle over my ex-husband's silent disapproval when I did something he didn't consider worthwhile. Living alone liberated me from that. I hadn't realised quite how much I'd let his way of thinking and being dominate my life.

Looking back, I can see that it wasn't always like that. In the early days, the pre-mortgage and pre-parenting days, there was less talk about money and savings and financial security. There was more focus on what we wanted, what would give us pleasure. And he did want to please me, to make me happy. I sometimes used to find notes on the windscreen of my car or under my pillow telling me how much he loved me.

The early days of a marriage.

Did it take long for me to adjust to living alone after the divorce? Did I miss the family home? Did I have moments of regret? Did I feel afraid? Was I concerned about my financial status as an older woman living alone?

The answer to all those questions was the same: no.

When I left, I left with a skip in my step and without looking back. And I still can't quite understand how it was so easy to leave, I really can't. Or why it took me so long. I think my focus for a long time had been caring; caring for my son and my ageing, needy parents. Getting a call in the middle of the night telling me that my eighty-year-old mother who spoke limited English had been found wandering along the freeway and had been taken to a local police station, or that my father had had a fall, or that she hadn't returned home since going shopping in the morning, or that they were locked out of the house on a thirty-plus degree day, or getting a call at work telling me that they were both in hospital after having had a car accident ... all of this didn't leave me much time for thinking about other things. I didn't have time for analysing my marriage and evaluating my level of satisfaction, emotional or otherwise. To put it simply, I was asleep in my life; every waking moment was taken up with other concerns.

After I made the decision to leave, a few friends expressed their concern for me; one made suggestions about what to do immediately after moving into my new home, telling me to keep busy in the first few months so that I wouldn't feel lonely. I didn't tell her that the only time I've ever felt really lonely was in the last few years of my marriage.

At the age of twenty, I had run away from home and from my controlling Italian mother. And at the age of fifty-seven, I ran away from home again. It felt like much the same thing, liberating. Everything fell into place effortlessly.

And I wasn't alone for long. I moved into my new house in May, and I was on an online dating site in July. It's not something I was planning to do; I didn't sit down and think, *I'm ready to meet someone, I want to meet someone, I'm going to join an online dating site.* No, it was my friend's twenty-five-year-old daughter who suggested it. She did more than that; she hopped online and set up an account for me on *RSVP*. All I had to do was provide the photos, including the mandatory full-length one – it seems size *does* matter – and then fill in my details. Easy.

But there was more, I had to create a profile. That took a while. I scrolled through other profiles to see what others had written, both men and women, and the photos they chose. One woman mentioned that she liked to 'look after her skin'. I wondered why she would include that. It's not something a prospective partner would need to know, and it was obvious anyway. She was in her early-sixties and she had a smooth, youthful complexion with no sign of wrinkles. That made me review my photos. What was I doing? Making comparisons, checking out my competition. Already I was beginning to question the whole thing. But I continued reading.

Some of the profiles read like a resume, and others like a job application, and some were very clear about what they were looking for and not looking for: 'No liars', 'Only contact me if you're looking for a long-term relationship', 'Please, only current photos!' and, 'No time wasters. I don't play games.'

It was obvious that some of these people had been on the site for a while, and were a bit wary of the pitfalls of online dating. I also realised it wasn't just a bio, I was going to have to 'sell' myself. The *How to Write Your Profile* advice I'd read online suggested that there was no need for an autobiography; just a few lines about what I like and what I don't like and what I'm looking for would be enough.

So, I listed a few likes: cosy dinners at home, walks in nature, reading and movies; and some dislikes – well, one in particular: noisy restaurants. And then I decided to be bold, to say what I really thought about online dating and meeting a potential partner – that it was an adventure. That's how I wanted to view it. Exploring unknown territory could be an adventure, and maybe someone out there might want to go on that adventure with me.

I'd noticed that some people used a catch line, like a hook. What was mine? 'Must love books.' I thought that would keep the illiterate away, and it might encourage other book lovers to connect. I even imagined evenings spent sitting on the sofa with my chosen one, reading our respective books and sometimes stopping to read a passage aloud to each other, something we both would delight in. Hmm, maybe that was a bit hopeful. A book lover and a good lover, that's what I really wanted. Again, hopeful.

I also had to include the age range of the men I was interested in meeting. I had to think about that for a moment. Could I see myself with a younger man? The newly-appointed French President, Emmanuel Macron, had been in the news recently, and I found myself reading about his personal life with great interest. He married a woman twenty-five years older, and she'd been his high school teacher. She divorced her husband of more than thirty years to marry him. When she turns eighty-five, he'll be sixty. I couldn't see how that would work. Well, they are French; that alone makes it more doable. But could *I*? I decided maybe a couple of years younger, but even that made me feel like I would be the older woman. I settled for late-fifties to early-sixties. I was fifty-seven at the time.

I told a few friends about my new adventure. All were encouraging, and a little curious. I knew they would be wanting regular updates once things got going. My friend Ian, an older man who had been married for almost forty years, had a very romantic view of love and would speak about it as being something you go towards knowing that it is a wonderful thing, but also something that encompasses both pain and loss. You can't shy away from that; it can't be avoided. When I told him about joining *RSVP* I saw the raised eyebrow and the intrigued smile. We talked about it for a while. He did know someone who had successfully met his current wife on a dating site, and then he gave me some very practical advice.

'Think of it like a job advertisement, you'll be attracting candidates that you'll have to interview to see if they meet your criteria for the job. And when it comes to the interview there are three questions that matter:

1. Tell me why you think you can do the job?
2. Will you be a good fit for the company?
3. Will you love the job?

And maybe one more: What do you think this organisation can give to you?'

The only thing missing was the request for referees. I had a bit of a chuckle at first, but then I realised that in the context of *RSVP* those questions could translate as:

1. What are your strengths and weaknesses?
2. Why do you think we would be compatible?
3. How do you see yourself as a partner?

All valid questions.

With my profile set up and ready to go, I sat back and waited for the 'kisses' to come in – a 'kiss' telling me that someone had checked my profile and considered me a potential partner, extending an invitation request to start a conversation, or something else. And as I discovered there was the 'something else'. But as I was also on the search for suitable matches, I would soon be sending out kisses of my own.

Chapter 2

I wasn't really comfortable with the process; scrolling through profiles, checking photos and making an assessment, or as Ian would suggest, asking whether he meets my criteria. It started to feel a bit like online shopping, with no refunds allowed. How was this going to go? Start an online chat, maybe a phone call or two, and then a meet up? I think that was the usual formula. And then there were the red flags, the warning signs that should never be ignored. But I'll get to those later.

I decided to be bold and start sending kisses before I received any. But there wasn't much that caught my eye. Yes, the profile shot was the first thing to get a tick, after that it really was a bit of guesswork. I'd read that the first phone call was an important step, but that there shouldn't be too many after that.

We start to form an idea of what someone looks like based on those conversations, sometimes an unrealistic one, and then inevitably disappointment follows at the first meeting. But the first meeting, that's what it was all leading to. While I was busy reading profiles and trying to make up my mind, the kisses started arriving.

Mark was the first to make contact. As a university tutor and fellow book lover, his profile made an interesting read, almost laid out like a novel. He mentioned his marriage breakup more than ten years ago, saying that at the time it seemed tragic but he'd since realised that the best things in his life had happened as a consequence. He went on to describe some of those things, which included travelling interstate and then overseas, where he lived and worked for a few years. His description of the places he'd been to, and the many and varied experiences he'd had along the way made me think that, yes, the interesting things that happened to him post-divorce wouldn't have happened to him had he stayed married.

He then spoke about treating people kindly and not having time for insincerity. He was caring and ready to put in the effort to make a relationship work. He was into meaningful conversations, good food, good art, walking in nature and along city laneways, good books, and sometimes writing. He tried to take pleasure in the small things and always looked for the extraordinary in the ordinary.

A very interesting man, a considerate man, and a like-minded person first up! He was also upfront and had a sense of playfulness, and I liked that very much. At the end, he presented an interesting request:

If you're finding it difficult to respond and feel like humouring me, tell me the three things you would do if you had superhuman powers. Or maybe tell me about the best thing that's happened to you recently. Or maybe just send me your phone number and we can talk instead, I'd like that. You probably don't need to find a pen pal, as I don't.

Okay, he was my first kiss, and I was ready and willing to return it – right away. And so, I did. After a short conversation online, an exchange of phone numbers followed. In a matter of days, we decided to meet up at a park not far from where I lived. This was my first meet up and I was feeling a little nervous.

I recognised him right away. He was sitting on a park bench with both arms stretched along the back, his legs stretched out in front and crossed at the ankles. He looked completely at ease, as I imagined he would. He liked being in nature and was a keen photographer of birds and wildlife, so meeting in the park was his idea. He turned to look my way when he noticed me approaching and he smiled a broad, welcoming smile. My first thought was, *phew*. And then I noticed his white shirt with the sleeves rolled up to the elbow, and the pale blue jeans – stylishly relaxed.

We sat on the bench and talked for over an hour and then we talked some more as we strolled around the park. He knew the names of the trees and flowers, and the myriad birds that were flying about. He seemed a real nature and animal lover, and gentle. We talked about the books we'd been reading and discovered we both had a thing for Anne Tyler, we'd read all her books and we shared our favourites. He told me he was thinking of retiring; he had plans to write the novel he'd always wanted to. He also had a keen interest in politics, which wasn't an interest we shared, but I feigned interest as I struggled to remember the name of our new Prime Minister.

I was surprised at how easy it was; after so many years of marriage, being with a stranger and imagining him naked in bed seemed very easy. There was something about him, his unhurried manner and the way he looked at me, that I found very sexy.

He was staying with friends while he decided where exactly he wanted to live. After his divorce, he didn't rush into buying another house; he wanted to explore his options, and enjoy his freedom for a while longer. And he had.

He had plans to go out for dinner with his friends that night, and that's what brought our meeting to an end. He walked me to my car and, as I was searching my bag for my keys, he placed his hand on my arm, looked at me and said, 'I want to see you again.'

Then he leaned forward and he kissed me – a brief kiss, but a soft, warm one. I felt the same way, so we made plans to meet again, a coffee in three days' time at a local café. As I was driving home, a message arrived on my phone from Mark:

[M] I so want to see you again. Not sure if I can wait.

An Interrupted Life

I was flattered, but I kept my cool and sent back a smiling emoji. I wasn't quite sure how to navigate this new terrain, and after my divorce, certainty was something I was trying to learn to do without. As a friend said, 'Just have fun.'

Three days later I was sitting in the courtyard at Mamma Says in Fairfield waiting for Mark. I was a little early, but I always am. I sat and waited. And waited. After half an hour and a cup of tea, I decided to send him a text:

> [I] I'm sitting at Mamma Says, but you're not here. I might have another cup of tea, you've probably been delayed, or you've changed your mind!

I decided humour was the best approach, it was too soon to be getting pissed off, and I wasn't anyway. I was enjoying sitting on my own and watching the other people around me, something I hadn't done in a long time. I waited a little while longer, but still no Mark. Later that night I got a very apologetic message telling me he hadn't checked his diary and had got the date wrong. He invited me to lunch to make up for it, a fancy Italian restaurant in the city. I thought I could do better:

> [I] Come to lunch at my place, I'll cook us an Italian dish.

I knew, of course, that inviting a stranger to my home was not what the online dating site recommended, but I'd checked out his Facebook page and with over 1000 friends, I thought he was low risk. And I liked him, I felt comfortable at our first meeting. He was a very attractive man, and I was still thinking about the kiss, gentle and inviting. But I did organise for a friend to call and check that all was going okay, at her suggestion.

I got busy checking recipes and decided an antipasto with a bowl of spaghetti pesto was the best way to go, simple and tasty. He was due at 11:00, I was still waiting at 12:00. Again, a no-show. Some might say that was a red flag, I thought it was just plain rude. And this time I told him; I sent a message telling him that I'd gone to the trouble of preparing lunch and I was looking forward to seeing him. His reply a short time later was again an apology, but a self-righteous one this time. He had to deal with a problem at the facility where he would now be storing his things while he was away, but at the same time, he didn't want anyone putting themselves out for him, ever.

He had told me that he would be travelling interstate to be closer to his elderly mother while she was ill, but I hadn't realised it was so soon. I wondered why he was pursuing me when he was putting his things in storage, something he hadn't mentioned. I wasn't sure how ill his mother was, but there was the real possibility he would be away for a long time. Where was his home base? I was beginning to think he didn't really know what he was doing, or what he wanted. And he seemed a bit preoccupied, and a bit forgetful.

I checked his Facebook page to see if his posts would tell me more about him. I saw that he was very much into politics and current affairs. His page was filled with pieces about Trump and China and homophobic *this* and Islamophobic *that*. Sometimes his posts went on and on, not just a paragraph or two, more like a thesis. It made me think about the male character in Meg Wolitzer's novel *The Wife* who was a very opinionated man about the politics of the time, but if he had to express an opinion about women he struggled to find anything to say. He lacked the understanding to be able to do so. I wondered if the same could be said about Mark.

I thought that would be the end of it, but later that night he sent a series of messages:

> [M] I'm sorry we didn't get to see each other. I wanted to see you, talk to you. Not that I had a great deal to say beyond the fact that I fancied you.
>
> [I] I was looking forward to seeing you too. Do you have any idea how long you'll be away? And Mark, you used the past tense.
>
> [M] At this stage I'm not sure. I think I just need to get her settled somewhere where she can be looked after. She can't be living alone anymore. Once that's done, I should be able to get back to Melbourne. And yes, I definitely fancied you and fancy you. If I'm being honest (and I am), I wanted and want to sleep with you, to hold you, to be close to you. I'm still not sure whether we're especially compatible in terms of what else we want from life, and what we might talk about, but you're that rare thing: someone I fancy.

I wasn't sure how to reply to his sudden burst of frankness; there was no deception and no pretence, he was very clear and honest. After a separation that had been anything but those things, I felt a sense of relief. But I wasn't sure it was a good idea to encourage the possibility of a relationship, or maybe even just sex, which is what he was really saying when he said he didn't think we'd have very much else in common, not even topics for conversation. That wasn't very encouraging. And we wouldn't even be living in the same state as he was going away, and soon. But he fancied me. He fancied *me*!

> [I] It sounds as though you're going to be occupied for a little while, and living interstate. And you might decide not to come back. Do you know of Brendon Grimshaw, the newspaper editor from Yorkshire? He bought an island and lived a long and happy life there surrounded by nature and wildlife. I think you might be a bit of a nomad too. That's also a rare thing.

His frankness continued:

> [M] Yes, but do you fancy me? Do you want to sleep with me?

I did think the chemistry was there at our first meeting, that first kiss. He was a very attractive man, even though he did walk with his shoulders slightly hunched and I had to keep resisting the urge to tell him to straighten up.

> [I] I don't have a lover at the moment, and I could do with one. And that could be you. But you're disappearing soon and that could be an impediment. Don't you think? This is my suggestion. After you know how long you'll be away, let me know and I'll come visit you. I will.

But he was in a hurry:

> [M] My alternative suggestion is that I could come and visit you, now.

The post-divorce sex had to happen sooner or later and I could have agreed and been bold, but I wasn't into casual sex. That's not what I wanted.

> [I] That is a possibility but you're leaving soon, not really a good idea. Get yourself settled, then we'll talk more about it.
>
> [M] Right you are then. I'll be leaving in a day or two, lots to do. But I'll be thinking of you.
>
> [I] And I'll be thinking of you.

And that's where it ended, both of us thinking.

Looking back, I sometimes wonder if things happen for a reason, one outcome averted in order for something else to happen, something that was meant to be. There are moments in our lives that only in hindsight we recognise as being pivotal ones. As Steve Jobs said, 'You can't connect the dots looking forward; you can only connect them looking backwards.'

Maybe everything does happen at exactly the right time and place, and whether we see it as synchronicity or coincidence, it doesn't matter. Maybe there is some order in the universe, or maybe it's just about timing – everything else perfect, but not at the right time. And that timing is the crucial point. That's how I now think about Mark, that I met him at the wrong time.

But not the others.

Chapter 3

Public servant Dan with a keen interest in literature, a fellow bookworm with a love of words, was my next kiss. It started with an email exchange where we shared favourite passages from books we had read; he sent one from *Mrs Dalloway*, I sent him one from *Olive Kitteridge*; I sent D. H. Lawrence, he sent Tolstoy.

And then we moved on to poems, *lots* of poems. It was an outdated way of getting to know one another, the way of 'letters', but I enjoyed it. And so did he. 'Already you have put a little excitement into my life,' he wrote in an email. That's when I thought it was time to meet.

I arrived at the café after him and I had a chance to check him out while he was looking at the menu. He looked older than sixty, but I didn't let that put me off. He was thin, with thin-rimmed glasses and a bit of a moustache that gave him the look of an academic, like one of my old English professors from university. His concentration on the menu was such that he could very well have been reading a novel, the way he was holding it open with both hands and looking completely absorbed by it.

We knew some things about each other, but communicating by email without the interference of pheromones and body language isn't the most reliable way to make an assessment of someone's character. I decided to have a cup of tea and a chat and see where it went – it was a chance to get to meet the real Dan. We'd talked books and poetry, now it was time to talk about ourselves, and it proved to be revelatory.

I knew he was separated – he'd mentioned that in his profile – but I didn't know he still *lived* with his wife. He was the *almost*-separated man. He explained that they lived very separate lives and that he was in the process of looking for somewhere else to live. I knew right away that wasn't going to work for me. But he tried to make me understand; this was his second marriage, a 'loveless marriage', as he put it. He said he'd probably been hasty in getting remarried so soon after his divorce, but after his first wife's infidelity he was feeling insecure. Having someone want him was reassuring and healing.

But it didn't last.

After some time, they stopped communicating and sleeping together. He started to feel alone in his marriage, and lonely for love. He yearned for the experience of a truly loving and romantic connection. And an intellectual one. Well, we had that, but I doubted that we'd have anything more; he was keen, very keen, but I wasn't. And he still referred to her as 'my wife'. That made me feel very uncomfortable.

Apart from his complicated domestic situation, he came across as a little needy and maybe overly sensitive. At one point we were talking about online dating not representing the real person, the person with weaknesses and vulnerabilities. I mentioned *Sophie's Choice* and the way Nathan and Sophie first meet in a library, where she's nervously asking an impatient librarian where she would find Emily Dickens – but I didn't get a chance to finish.

At the mention of the book, I heard an intake of breath and he suddenly made a strange sound, like a stifled sob. The next thing I knew, he was quietly crying. It was a story that moved him to tears, just at the mention of it. I felt bad, but I was also stunned.

What I wanted to say, but didn't get a chance to, was that the librarian's hostile response to Sophie getting Emily Dickinson's name wrong caused her to faint and then vomit into Nathan's hand. He comforted her and berated the librarian, and they went on to fall in love. But of course, with tragic consequences. My point would have been that it wasn't the most romantic first meeting, her vomiting in his hand. But with my first meeting with Dan ending with him in tears, perhaps theirs wasn't so bad.

The emails continued after the meeting, and I didn't mind the intellectual exchange, but I was reluctant to see him again. I did tell him that I wasn't comfortable with his domestic situation but he remained optimistic – until I refused to have another meeting.

Suddenly, the cultured, urbane Dan disappeared, and I saw the other Dan, the uncouth Dan. Maybe they can coexist, maybe it isn't so shocking to have different aspects to our personalities, but I saw a split personality – a huge red flag. And maybe overly sensitive, another red flag:

> **[D]** Here's the deal, we talk and we fuck. We've done enough talking.

His message almost made me laugh; it was so ridiculous. I could have ignored it but decided to send a final message:

> **[I]** It was nice meeting you, all four of you: the cultured Dan, the stylish Dan, the sensitive Dan, and the uncouth Dan. Yes, there was an uncouth Dan waiting to be discovered.

Some time passed before a message arrived telling me that he was now living alone and this:

> **[D]** I await a poem.

He would be waiting a long time.

Charles's photo was very appealing, a handsome man with a full head of hair, and a lovely smile. His first message addressed some of the things I mentioned in my profile; here was someone who was paying attention.

He started by agreeing with me that choosing a life partner could be like going on an adventure. I liked that he referred to that.

And then he elaborated:

[C] I see that we share an interest in walking in nature, reading, music, movies (I have just been to eleven movies at MIFF), cosy dinners at home and cats, although having had a string of ginger cats in my life and one Russian Blue. I don't have a cat in my life at the moment, as I enjoy the feeling of freedom of being cat-free. I also love going to talks at the Wheeler Centre, and classical music concerts.

I'd enjoy hearing back from you, whatever you would like to share. Are you still working? I'm not, I have what is called a 'portfolio of interests'. How many children do you have, and what ages are they?

With warm regards, Charles

My first thought was, *Eleven movies? I don't think I could find more than one I would want to go and see at the moment.* But he was very polite and friendly, and, as with Dan, another long online conversation developed. Again, a conversation about books read, about writing, and about films, classical music, cats, and walks in nature. We covered quite few topics. He seemed an interesting man and so I suggested we have a phone conversation.

[C] Rather than talking on the phone, would you like to meet for a coffee over the weekend sometime? One suggestion would be the Fairfield Boathouse, 11am on Saturday. We could meet at the entrance, near the barbecue area.

No phone numbers were exchanged.

I got there early and waited at the entrance of the boathouse. I recognised him right away, a tall man wearing a smart blazer over casual pants; not exactly walking attire, but stylish. I was wearing my faded three-quarter length jeans with the obligatory rips just above the knee and a tight-fitting black t-shirt. We weren't matched fashion-wise, but so far, intellectually we were.

We sat at a table overlooking the river and talked for an hour, mostly about our reading and our writing projects, and then we decided to stay and have lunch.

Why not?

It was perfect weather and he seemed like perfect company, very relaxed and a good listener; he seemed genuinely interested in what I had to say. He didn't elaborate on the 'portfolio of interests' he'd mentioned in his message. He asked about my son, he wanted to know his age and if he lived with me. He seemed relieved when I told him he was living independently. I guessed then that he didn't have children, and I was right. He'd had cats instead.

I ordered something simple, a bowl of oven-baked chips, and he had the classic burger with a salad. I wasn't all that hungry, and it was a huge bowl. I only had a few and, being polite, I offered him some, which he happily accepted. The burger with chips was probably a better combination than burger and salad. It was time to leave and he suggested splitting the bill. I was a little surprised. I didn't mind paying my share, but he had eaten most of my chips. For some reason that bothered me. Maybe not what I expected from such a well-mannered, well-dressed man. There was just a brief hug when we said goodbye and we agreed to talk soon.

We continued our chats on the dating site, no phone calls. When I suggested we move to emails, he ignored the suggestion. So, I questioned it:

> [I] You prefer to talk on RSVP rather than via email?
>
> [C] Yes, for some reason communicating through RSVP feels good. Hope this is okay for you.

Huh? Feels good? I didn't quite understand why. He had said that we shouldn't reveal too much about ourselves too soon, that things should emerge in a 'natural way'. At the time I didn't stop to question it, because he had gone on to say that 'being with someone in a truly intimate way takes time, because it reveals ourselves in a way that nothing else does. We become fellow travellers.'

True intimacy, fellow travellers ... he was speaking my language. But after his stubborn reluctance to talk outside *RSVP* I realised that he didn't want me to know his surname, or have his phone number. I began to wonder what it was he was hiding. He wanted to remain anonymous. If it was in a kinky sex context, I might have understood, but it was beginning to feel a little creepy. Yes, creepier than the kinky sex scenario. Suddenly, I felt very uncomfortable, and I let him know:

> [I] Dear Charles, I'm not sure I understand your reluctance to have a conversation outside RSVP. It feels a little odd. We've met face-to-face but we can't communicate via email. And I can't know your surname or phone number.

I understand what you say about things emerging in a 'natural way', but somehow this doesn't feel at all natural. Oh, well.

Kind regards, Ida

I wasn't too surprised when I didn't get a reply.

The next few encounters didn't even make it to a face-to-face meeting.

Adrian worked as a civil engineer and also loved reading, and sometimes writing. He sent me a kiss but didn't wait for me to accept, the usual step before a conversation started. Instead, I saw a chat box appear at the bottom of my screen and a 'Hello' message from Adrian. I wasn't sure how he could do that; I'd never seen it happen, but it might have had something to do with his premium membership privileges. I was surprised but impressed that he was prepared to take the plunge and not do the 'wait and see' thing.

And that's how his messages began; brief to start with, and then long, detailed messages that included some of his writing. It was as if he needed to expel the words he had inside, words that had been accumulating for a long time and had to find an outlet. When I asked him if he went to such lengths when chatting with other members, he told me that his work didn't always give him an opportunity to enjoy the 'pleasures of intelligent conversation'. And that's what we were having, an intelligent conversation. He also graciously acknowledged that everyone on the site was busy with their lives:

[A] It behooves us to make an effort; to try and make interesting conversation and to engage in a genuine manner. On a more practical note, by putting in some effort at this point, we demonstrate that we might be the sort of person who will put in effort later on. Also, the fact is this is a sales pitch and we have to make ourselves attractive, otherwise … No sale, thank you sir. Next customer please. And it does take effort, especially as in this case when typing on a phone with two thumbs.

Well, that explained the numerous spelling mistakes. Being a teacher, my first impulse was to correct in red and return. And I wasn't sure his sales pitch was working for me; I wasn't persuaded to try the product, yet. Maybe it was after he sent me a list of some of his favourite books that I started to have my doubts: *The Phantom Tollbooth* by Norton Juster, Dr Seuss, *Dune* by Frank Herbert, *The Moon is a Harsh Mistress* by Robert Heinlein, *Eloise in Moscow* by Kay Thompson, all of Scott Turow's books, and Mrs Beeton's *Book of Household Management*.

There was nothing there that I would be interested in reading. Science fiction isn't a genre I enjoy although his inclusion of children's books did make me smile. But he persisted, and his messages grew even longer, almost essay-like.

He seemed an interesting man, a book lover who enjoyed cooking and giving massages. That wasn't a bad combination. And he seemed to enjoy the written exchange. I liked that about him; he wasn't in a hurry to move things along. But after a while, reading his messages started to take up a lot of time, and there were other applicants to respond to. I wasn't sure that I could sustain a conversation on the topics that interested him. He seemed to talk about himself – a lot. It might have been that he was trying to impress me, or a sign that he was self-centred, or maybe even insecure. It was only after several pages of autobiography that he finally asked about me:

> **[A]** Tell me something about yourself. I know you have an unsociable cat, and that you like books, but there must be more to you than that.

But my enthusiasm was beginning to wane. I told him that I'd enjoyed our exchange but I was feeling a little overwhelmed and I was going to slow down for a bit. He apologised for his ramblings and left his number just in case I changed my mind because, as he put it, 'Phone calls take up less time than typing.' And I had to agree with that, the typing was becoming tedious. Maybe a phone call at the start might have led to a different conclusion. Yes, the maybes – there were plenty of those.

Then came Brendan. A gentle-looking man with a greying beard who spent a lot of time at his local library because he was having problems with his internet connection at home. After a very short exchange online, I knew that he lived alone in a house full of clutter with worms for pets. He had a strong interest in music and books and was thinking of joining a book group. But he wasn't comfortable chatting online:

[B] Think I will sign off now because this is a very uncomfortable place. Will leave you my phone number and hope to hear from you.

He seemed a bit nervous, and a solitary sort of person. I didn't need to talk to him to realise that we really didn't have much in common. The cluttered house alone was, for me, a very large red flag. An odd man, but a gentle one nonetheless.

Steve was another man who preferred to talk on the phone rather than spend time writing messages. I was beginning to realise it was definitely easier. I would have to give my phone number out early on, but after just one phone call I would know if there was the possibility of more. Steve did send one message:

[S] Dear Ida, how wonderful that we both value compassion and adventure, a relationship adventure! Your lovely smile got my attention right away and from reading your profile, I see you are truly delightful and interesting. Yes, I think we might have much in common, so let's talk and we'll find out. If we enjoy the chat, we could arrange to meet. I'm looking forward to getting to know you. Sweet dreams, Steve.

A flattering message, perhaps intentionally so, but I sent him my number.

Well, one phone call really was enough. Steve was very clear about what he was looking for, an 'independent' woman who wouldn't 'hijack' his life. He'd dated needy women who couldn't function well on their own and demanded a lot of his time. He was very direct, and he got that out the way right away. He'd also dated women with children living at home, even adult children, and that caused conflict in the relationship. The adult children resented his presence in their mother's life; they didn't like her choice of partner and made it very clear. And the women always put their children's needs above their own. I listened without judging and I then told him that I had a son. Without hesitating he asked, 'How old is your son? Does he live with you?' Another man relieved to hear that my son lived independently, and the conversation moved on.

Even though he seemed genuine and I sort of understood where he was coming from, I didn't think he was very understanding of a mother's role. And why didn't those adult children like him? I got the impression that he was a little stubborn in his thinking, and maybe a little demanding. Maybe those adult children saw this too.

The next kiss I received was from Chris, a younger man – a *much* younger man. He was only thirty years old. That would make our age difference even greater than the age difference between President Macron and his wife. He was smiling in his photo and he looked like a lovely young man. I couldn't think of him as sexy or handsome, it didn't feel right. He could have been one of my son's friends. I was curious as to why he would be sending a kiss to a much older woman, and I was tempted to ask him, but maybe it wasn't so hard to understand. It wasn't exactly gerontophilia, and just as younger women can be attracted to older men, the reverse also made sense. I always found myself drawn to older men and had crushes on one of my school teachers, and then my much older English professor. Ah yes, I remember that well. The way my professor used to look at me in tutorials, I was pretty certain the feeling was mutual. But he was a married man.

Jack was the closest I got to dating a psycho. As harsh as that sounds, one phone conversation was enough to make me realise that he wasn't quite normal. He introduced himself briefly online and left me his number asking me to call. And so I did. After the initial chit chat, I said it was a good idea to talk right away and not spend time messaging. His reply was a bit odd, 'I don't want to *talk*, I want to have a conversation'.

He emphasised the word 'talk' as if it was an offensive suggestion. But I gave him the benefit of the doubt, thinking he meant he was into more meaningful conversations, which suited me fine. He asked me about the origins of my name and when he heard I was Italian he started talking about food. I didn't mind that as a topic of conversation either.

'I love Italian food,' he told me.

'Really? I make my own pasta. Do you like ravioli, homemade?'

'I make my own pasta, too.'

Not the reply I expected, but I continued.

'I'm impressed. Do you use a pasta machine? I have one, but it's unused and still in its box. I prefer a rolling pin; the old-fashioned method. I still have the one my mother used to use.'

'I use a rolling pin too,' he replied.

It was beginning to sound like a contest, who's the more skilled pasta maker.

'Really? Not many people I know do. Do you manage to get thin sheets of dough? That can be a bit tricky. And I don't like thick pasta, too chewy.'

'I don't have a problem at all; I can roll the sheets very thin. I can probably make better pasta dough than your mother or your nonna could make.'

WTF? Is this guy a loon or what?

But I tried to go on, to change the subject, get off dangerous pasta-making territory and talk about something else. I tried to ask about his daughter – turns out she was also a skilled pasta maker. I tried again to veer off the subject, but he kept interrupting me. After several attempts to have a reasonable 'conversation', he stopped me mid-sentence with, 'You're not listening to me.'

That's when I decided I'd had enough. 'Jack, are you listening to me?'

'Of course I am.'

'Then listen to this.'

And that's when I ended the call.

I didn't have to stop and listen to my gut instinct; the message was coming through loud and clear. *Stay away, this guy is a weirdo.*

That's when I Googled 'online dating survival guides'. I needed help. There were a few and they listed the red flags to look out for, the warning signs that shouldn't be ignored: the player looking for sex, with lots of women; the very needy, recently divorced man who can't function on his own; the 'almost-separated' man still living with his wife; the never-married older man who hasn't had a serious relationship; the non-monogamous man who's into open relationships; the 'juggler' who's dating several women at the same time just to keep his options open; the too-good-to-be-true man who is smart, successful, charming, and likes everything about you; the fast-mover who declares his love after the first date and is ready to cohabit; and the liar, the man who's ten years older and a good twelve inches shorter than what he posted on his online profile.

Apart from Jack, and Dan the almost-separated man, I hadn't come across any glaring red flags; but then, I hadn't been on many dates, either. Most of the men I encountered all had one thing in common: a need for connection, and loneliness – even within a marriage. And that's not what I was expecting. There was the possibility of maintaining a friendship with some of those men, and I could do with a few more male friendships. But it wasn't what I was looking for.

Chapter 4

After only a short time I was already considering closing my account and leaving things to chance, or fate. A friend had told me about a woman she knew and that woman's chance encounter, and I've never forgotten it. She had been walking along the beach early one morning and she noticed a man having trouble with his paraglider. He was struggling and falling. She watched, helpless, as he fell from the sky almost at her feet. He was slightly injured; she was a nurse. They've been together ever since.

Maybe that's what I wanted, a man falling at my feet. But then I remembered something else my friend had told me, to 'just have fun'. And that's what I wasn't having, not yet. So, I decided it was my turn to send out a kiss. Rather than respond, I would be doing the searching.

It was his photo that caught my attention. Yes, that was the first thing everybody looked at and ticked off, but something about his smile – his *almost* smile – had *me* smiling. It was a kind face, and there was a hint of something else: sensuality. It wasn't overt, it was just suggested in that smile, and both his hands were in the front pockets of his jeans. His profile was brief and made a mention of integrity and intelligent conversation, something he thought was in short supply, but he wasn't giving too much away – not even his name. He had an unusual username, Kefir. I wasn't sure what the connection between a fermented milk drink and this man could be, but I sent a kiss and got a kiss in return. The door was open for introductions. After my recent experiences, I thought a bit of humour would be a good way to start:

> **[I]** Hello, shall we start an intelligent conversation? Kidding, just a conversation. But that comment on your profile did make me smile. RSVP tells me that we're an eighty-eight per cent match. That's the first time I've hit the eighties, it's usually around the fifties. Not very encouraging, but then people have told me my profile is a little incomplete. Another thing about your profile that I liked, very much, you use the word 'integrity'. That is a big deal.
>
> I don't know your name, but I'd like to.
>
> Ida

His reply came the next morning, early on a Saturday:

> **[J]** Hi Ida, I actually heard that comment about 'intelligent conversations' from a woman I had a meet up with. I don't pay much attention to the ratings on this site. I think they just put that stuff on there to give the impression that they've used some scientific formula to assess compatibility. My name is Jev.

Well, he missed the humour about the stats and he was to the point, no ramblings, and no questions or elaborations or essays. The first thing I did was Google his name; it was unusual and I'd never heard it before. I found that it was an abbreviation of the name Jevan, and that it comes from the Welsh name Evan. Well, one thing I did know about Jevan was that he was a man of few words. I wasn't used to that and I wasn't sure how to proceed. Should I wait and see if he delivered more? Or should I keep chatting and ask some open-ended questions? I considered borrowing Mark's question, 'What would you do if you had super human powers?' But I wasn't sure he was really interested. Maybe he was just being polite by returning the kiss. His response wasn't exactly encouraging. But proceed, I did:

> **[I]** Hi Jev, I don't pay much attention to the ratings either. I haven't been on RSVP for long and it's all new to me. But a conversation is a different thing. Do you have conversations online or do you prefer to talk on the phone?

The message had been 'Seen' at 1.04pm, but he didn't respond right away. I waited and checked – that's what you do on these sites, keep checking. By 6.30pm I couldn't resist:

> [I] People say a lot on their profiles, sometimes too much. I think faces say more. Yours does.

His reply came almost right away:

> [J] I prefer to talk on the phone, and then if that goes well to actually meet up.

That was it, no suggestion of calling, no number left. His aloofness was a bit of a challenge. So, I gave it another try, this time his style:

> [I] Yes, that makes sense.

Seen at 6.45pm and then silence. Sunday late afternoon, I decided to be bold and send my number. That got an instant response:

> [J] Thanks, I'm tied up this evening but I'd like to ring and have a chat tomorrow night around 8pm, if that suits you?

Okay, he was interested in having a conversation – I had to remember that. Start with sending a kiss, then a message, then comes the phone call, and then maybe a meet up. That's when all is revealed.

He called the following night and we spoke for half an hour, a good conversation that flowed without any awkward moments. He told me he was an English teacher, as I was, and that immediately felt like a connection. And as an English teacher, I didn't have to worry about him not loving books.

We talked about teaching and, to my surprise, I discovered that after thirty years he still enjoyed being in the classroom. Well, he enjoyed the interaction with young people, but not the marking and report writing and the admin.

He was also a musician and had played guitar in a band in New Zealand, where he was born, before becoming a teacher. He'd also recorded some songs with a local singer he teamed up with and they put together a couple of CDs. He still played now, but only with friends. I liked the sound of his voice. It was smooth, easy to listen to, and even though he grew up in New Zealand he had no trace of a Kiwi accent. He seemed to be enjoying our conversation, but in a contained sort of way. He wasn't as gushing as the others, or in a rush. He seemed very laid back. At the end of the call we didn't make arrangements to meet, he didn't suggest it and neither did I, instead he suggested another call soon.

I wanted to meet him, but I didn't want to be the one to initiate it, as I did the first phone call. I had just recently read *The Subtle Art of Not Giving a F*ck* by Mark Manson. If I adopted Manson's 'I don't give a fuck' approach to the little things in life that bother us, and particularly in the face of the inevitability of death, I shouldn't give in to fear, or any other negative emotion.

So, what would I do? I'd tell Jev that I liked him. That he had a seductive voice. That I had been thinking of him. That I'd like to meet him and get to know him better. And that whatever happens, happens.

But I wasn't quite there yet. So instead, I tested the waters. He'd told me that he often visited Northcote because his son lived there; he lived in Healesville, an hour's drive from the city. I decided on just a bit of a nudge:

> [I] I was in Northcote yesterday shopping at Terra Madre (I can't stay away) and browsing second-hand bookshops. Maybe we'll run into each other in Northcote, in a bookshop.

Again, an almost instant response and finally a suggestion to meet up:

> [J] I go to Terra Madre too, when I'm visiting my son. Their rye bread is pretty damn good. We can meet for a coffee without waiting to randomly run into each other.
>
> [I] I like that idea even better. Let me know when you're free.
>
> [J] Will do … heading into some pretty heavy marking but maybe the weekend after this upcoming one, if you're interested then.
>
> [I] Sounds good. Send me a text message closer to the time and let me know which day suits – or call.

Finally, we had arranged to meet. But then what followed were days of silence, which I thought was a bit odd. We could have continued some sort of conversation before the meet up, online or by text. I was still getting messages from other men, and I was replying. I was having conversations with them, but not with Jev. I decided to share something I'd read with him. No chit chat, just a comment that could lead to a discussion, an intellectual discussion:

> **[I]** I read something yesterday: 'The magnificent thing, however, is that you don't have to understand all things. The end of every thought process does not have to be a conclusion, that's just an essay and life is not an essay.' I like that, thought you might too.

Then I waited, keen to hear his take on it, and to possibly get a conversation going.

> **[J]** I haven't finished an actual thought since 1979.

That was it, one brief sentence. And it was either true or it was his quirky sense of humour, I wasn't sure which. So, I gave it another try:

> **[I]** I picked up a book at The Book Grocer in Northcote last time I was there, The Subtle Art of Not Giving a Fu*k by Mark Manson. I think this book is going to be a very interesting experience. He says that when you learn to not give a fuck about things, when you just let things be, they have a way of falling into place on their own. And he doesn't mean indifference. I hope you've had a good day.
>
> **[J]** What does he mean if not giving a fuck isn't indifference?

Okay, another solitary sentence, but now I had the invitation to elaborate:

> [I] What he says is that most people think that not giving a fuck means being indifferent, but that's not it. He goes on to say that the key to a good life is to only give a fuck about things that matter and are important. Everything else has to go. It's about learning how to decide what truly matters based on our values. And then there's acceptance. Once we start accepting instead of wanting to change things, we learn to embrace our fears and our insecurities. We learn to live more courageously. And we shouldn't feel bad about feeling bad, that's what he means by not giving a fuck.

I don't think I'd ever used the f-word so many times in one paragraph, it was strangely exhilarating.

> [J] So, only give a fuck about what's important? That's not as easy as it sounds. I recently bought a book, also at The Book Grocer, about thinking less, and doing less. I've just started reading it. I'll let you know
> …

The conversation stopped there; I didn't reply. There wasn't much I could say about a book he hadn't read yet, and I wasn't going to waste my time trying to come up with engaging topics for discussion. I'd leave that for the classroom.

The next few days passed in silence, waiting for the weekend meet up. We hadn't decided on which day or where we'd meet. By Friday I was beginning to think he might have changed his mind, or forgotten. I wasn't sure which one was worse; either he didn't find me interesting or he was unreliable. By Saturday evening I had to find out which it was. I decided to be direct:

> [I] I thought we had agreed to have a coffee this weekend, an arranged meeting not a random one in a bookshop. But since I haven't heard from you, I assume that's not going to be happening now. If I adopt the 'I don't give a fuck' approach to life, what would I do? I would tell you that something about your photo caught my attention, and my interest. I would tell you that you have a seductive voice. I would tell you that I've been thinking of you and that I'd like to get to know you better. And then whatever happens, happens.

I didn't have to wait long for his reply:

> [J] We could meet tomorrow. I could be out your way by late morning.

No explanation, no apology, no excuses. I decided to leave the message unanswered for a while; it was his turn to wait. But I knew I'd be agreeing.

We arranged to meet the next day, he was going to catch the train in and I would be picking him up at the station at 11.00am. It was just up the road from my place. There wasn't much time to prepare, or to worry, and that probably worked out for the best. I didn't have time to try on different outfits and agonise over what to wear, or to go to the hairdresser.

I decided to wear jeans with boots and a long-sleeved top – it was the end of winter and the days were still a little cold. My hair, which I had stopped colouring, was streaked with grey, but evenly at the front. Some people thought I had intentionally bleached it that way. I was just tired of the effort involved in the almost monthly touch-ups, and happy to accept the notion of graceful ageing.

After constantly checking myself in the mirror, and the time, I grabbed my cars keys and headed to the station.

Chapter 5

I got to the station ten minutes before the train arrived. I paced the platform trying to decide the best place to wait. I wanted to be able to see him get off without being seen, and of course I had no way of knowing where that would be, or if he'd look like he did in his picture. I decided to wait at the entrance and then I'd move out once the train arrived. I would be the one visible to him, though, as being on the train gave him the advantage.

The loudspeaker announced the arrival time and I edged my way closer to the platform. I waited as the train came to a halt and several doors slid open at the same time. I stood carefully watching an assortment of people getting off.

My focus was on the men – a man with a cane, a very short man, a very overweight man, a too young man, and then I saw him – the only man that I thought could be him, the one I hoped was him. As we walked towards each other, I couldn't help but smile: he was wearing mirrored sunglasses. Clever, he could check me out without me noticing. Good strategy.

But because of the glasses there wasn't that first moment of eye contact, that immediate connection that I would be able to remember down the track. I had no choice but to focus on his body instead, which I did. He was tall and lean, with cropped greying hair, a stubble beard, and long legs. He was wearing a blue denim jacket with the collar turned up and black jeans, and he had a red backpack slung over his shoulder. No disappointments so far, but the glasses had to come off, and then they did. He was just like his photo, a gentle face with a hint of a smile, a sensuous smile.

'Hi there,' he said, and again that small smile.

'Hi,' I said, as I adjusted my gaze to his face, now with eye contact. Then we did a quick kiss hello on both cheeks, Italian style.

He seemed completely relaxed, like someone who had been on a few dates and had met other women on railway platforms before. I wasn't good at arranged first meetings; I was better at spontaneous ones. I could initiate conversations with strangers I'd just met on the street, in the park, in a supermarket – no problem. This was very different, an anxiety-filled different.

Since no plans had been made, I suggested we go for a walk at the Darebin Parklands nearby, and then perhaps a coffee somewhere afterwards. He liked the idea as he'd been sitting for over an hour on the train and didn't particularly want to sit in a café right away. I had recently discovered the parklands and tried to walk there most days. It had become an early morning ritual, a good way to start the day. Sometimes a good way to end the day, as well, particularly if it had been a difficult one. In nature, I had discovered the antidote to stress. And on a first date it was far less stressful than sitting across a table trying to interpret what every expression really meant; walking and talking seemed the perfect combination.

It was a five-minute drive and during that time we exchanged the usual preliminary chitchat about the train ride and the convenience of having a station at the end of my street, and the parklands nearby. He told me he had marked some essays while he was on the train, and then we shared the teacher's common lament about endless marking and report writing. He'd moved the car seat right back to accommodate his long legs, which I noticed were stretched all the way out. I was glad to be driving; to be doing something made me a little less self-conscious, and less likely to talk too quickly and gesticulate – something non-Italians interpret as anxiety.

When we got to the parklands we walked for a bit and then sat on at a bench overlooking the creek under the shade of a gum tree. And we talked. He told me about his experiences with online dating. It was a subject that came up with the others too, a sort of *let's compare notes*. Jev told me he'd had one long-term relationship after his divorce that lasted just over a year, and since then he'd been on several dates, and had some casual sex. He spoke about 'servicing' an Asian woman; well, that's what he discovered she wanted – just sex. Her husband wasn't interested in exploring her erotic needs and was hasty even with his own. And because of that she was initially nervous and insecure, but she knew what she wanted. She wanted to experience pleasure and that's what she got, orgasm after orgasm.

He then described sex with a Mediterranean woman being like a 'playground', nothing was off-limits – role-play, bondage, blindfolds, the works. I was a little surprised at how easily he talked about his sexual encounters. He was very matter-of-fact, without any awkwardness or hesitation or embellishment. And on a first date. But he wasn't boasting about his exploits in the bedroom, he was simply recounting what his recent experiences had been, and what he was expecting instead. He made a point of telling me that casual sex wasn't what he was looking for, not even during his pre-marriage years playing in a band and travelling around New Zealand. But it's what the older women he'd met online seemed to want. Or, as he put it, 'regular sex on a casual basis'.

He was the one feeling used. I'd never thought of men feeling that way, and it surprised me that he did. I always imagined women to be the ones wary of men who were only after casual sex. But not these women – they were middle-aged women, happy with just having a physical relationship. They weren't interested in anything more, and they kept coming back for more. They'd had the career, the marriage, the family, the duties and responsibilities, the sometimes-perfunctory sex that comes with a long-term marriage, and then the divorce. Just as I'd had. And they weren't prepared to follow all that with a solitary, sexless old age. They knew what they wanted, they wanted to explore their own needs in the bedroom. And Jev was happy to accommodate, for a while.

Then I asked him if he'd ever experienced the spiritual element in sex, something I'd discovered in my reading of D. H. Lawrence when I was at school. He didn't reply but he looked at me with what I can only describe as curiosity, and then he turned his gaze towards the trees on the other side of the creek as if he was giving it some thought. And we sat in silence for a while, just looking at the trees and listening to the sound of the creek bubbling over the rocks and fallen branches. But it was a comfortable stillness. Magpies and currawongs were calling in the distance, and dogs were barking at the nearby dog park; it was very easy to sit and just be still.

I can't remember how the next subject came up, but he mentioned that he'd cut a girlfriend's hair.

'You know how to cut women's hair?'

'When I lived in New Zealand my girlfriend was a hairdresser and she taught me, so I could cut her hair.'

And then I noticed his hands, slender with long fingers. Beautiful hands, hands that know how to hold a pair of scissors in one and a comb in the other. I couldn't help but wonder how many kisses he'd have received if he'd included that piece of information on his dating profile.

'My hairdresser decided to do the tree change thing and moved 120kms away from the city, and me,' I said, 'and I haven't been able to find anyone to replace him. He'd been my hairdresser for almost twenty years.'

'Yeah, I get that. It's an important relationship, and it's a trust thing, too.'

The all-important relationship women have with their hairdresser is well known. I've often thought that if it's good, if your hairdresser knows you and your hair, then it's pretty much irreplaceable. Mine knew all about my hair and about me. When he moved, I couldn't start looking for a replacement right away, it seemed almost disloyal. That and there was a sense of loss, maybe more than I felt at the end of my marriage. I noticed him looking at my hair, but it was held up by a large clip.

'Is your hair very long?' he asked.

I loosened the clip and let my hair fall over my shoulders. 'It's long, and needs a trim. And a colour, but I've decided I'm going to let the grey grow out. I've been thinking about it for a while and now seems like the right time. No hairdresser, no colour.'

He reached across and gently ran his hand through my hair, as if he was assessing it.

'What do you think?' I asked.

'It's in good condition and I like the grey streaks at the front. It looks as though you've had it professionally done.'

It was the most sensuous thing, his hand through my hair. I don't think he knew the effect it had; he was simply assessing the condition. But I couldn't stop thinking that *this man running his hand through my hair ... this man is going to cut my hair*. I imagined a scene befitting a tale from Greek mythology, but not with the same tragic consequences. Then he commented on my jeans, he liked them. I was impressed that he'd noticed, and that he told me. I liked them too. They were straight leg cut and a slim fit, and they were comfortable.

Maybe it was being out in the open surrounded by trees, but I was feeling completely relaxed, not like the other times. And it didn't take me long to decide that I was going to break the online dating rule of never having a first date come to your home. So, instead of going to a café, I invited him back to my place for a cup of tea. He looked at me as if he was trying to read my real intention. But he didn't ask questions, he happily accepted. By the time we got there it was early afternoon and I offered to prepare something to eat. He seemed genuinely appreciative, and he offered to help. He cut up the breadstick and I prepared the prosciutto and feta cheese and olives – staple items in my fridge.

We sat in my courtyard and ate lunch and talked some more. I told him about an Elizabeth Strout novel I'd just finished reading, he told me about an Australian drama series he'd just finished watching. He grabbed a pen from his shirt pocket and wrote the name of the series, *Mystery Road*, on a piece of paper that was sitting on the table and suggested I watch it. As he continued talking, he kept the pen in his hand and tapped it on the piece of paper, almost in tempo to his words. *A true musician.*

We talked more about school and work and our experiences with the education system. He was working full-time, I worked as a casual relief teacher. He asked me if I enjoyed it.

'Well, I don't have all the responsibilities of a regular teacher and that's something I don't miss. I'm a visitor and I get to interact with the students in a different way. Sometimes it can be very productive, and fun.'

'How do you mean?'

'When there's been no work left, and that does happen, I have to improvise. I always go for creative writing; the students always enjoy that. I give them a topic and they have free rein, and the results can be surprisingly good. I enjoy reading their work and they enjoy sharing it. It's a change from the more structured classwork they're used to.'

'Yeah, I can see how that would work, for you and the students. You should come and do some relief teaching at my school.'

'If the travel time were shorter, I'd consider that.'

He told me about his move to Australia from New Zealand after he got married; I told him about my time living in Italy before I got married. We both had long-term marriages that ended, his six years ago, mine just over a year. We talked about our children. He had two sons, one living and working overseas and the other living in Melbourne. I told him about my son, who was studying to be a doctor. We talked about family, we both had one sister. He was estranged from his and hadn't spoken to her in over a year. I told him I had a similar episode with my sister but things were better now. We agreed that these things happen in families all the time.

'You might reconnect with your sister at some point. But one of you will have to initiate that.'

'I'm not sure that's going to happen anytime soon.'

I didn't ask why and he didn't elaborate, he just changed the subject. He told me had an autoimmune condition that was slow in progressing and that the only cure was a liver transplant. But he wasn't expecting that any time soon, and I didn't really give it a second thought.

I offered him a cup of tea and that's when he noticed the lemons growing on the espaliered trees behind him and suggested putting a slice in his tea. They were Meyer lemons but he wasn't familiar with them, and neither was I until I moved in. They were a combination between a mandarin and a lemon. He liked the flavour and so I picked a few for him to take home. And then he looked at his watch and he was surprised to find that it was 4:00, almost time to catch the train back to Healesville. I offered to drive him to the station so he didn't have to rush. As he was collecting his things, he thanked me for lunch and asked if he could reciprocate, maybe next weekend. I accepted his invitation.

I pulled up just outside the station but there wasn't time to get out and walk him to the platform.

'So, see you next weekend?' This time his smile was wide; even his eyes were smiling.

'Yes, I'm looking forward to coming to Healesville, and my haircut!'

He was still smiling, a smile that seemed to be hinting at something more, when he reached for the door handle. But I stopped him. I took his arm and drew him close to me, and then we kissed. He didn't seem surprised; it was as if he was waiting for me to make the first move. And I was glad I did.

When I got home, he'd sent a text:

> [J] I forgot to take the lemons!
>
> [I] Don't worry, I'll bring them when I come next weekend.

Thinking about it later, I realised that when I first saw Jev walking towards me on the railway platform, the feeling that had rushed through me was one of familiarity, of recognition. It was as if we already knew each other, and were now meeting again after a time apart. Yes, he felt familiar, like someone I'd known before.

When? Where? That I couldn't say. Had I believed in reincarnation, I might have thought in another life.

Chapter 6

I arrived at Healesville just after 10:00 on a Saturday morning. I'd been up since 5:00 trying to decide what to wear; long-sleeved top or blouse, jeans or leggings, heels or walking boots. And trying to decide if lipstick was appropriate for the country. I decided, yes.

As I drove along his street, I noticed the views of the hills on one side of the road, the side Jev's house was on. I saw his letterbox on the footpath before I saw his house. It was a sloping block and his weatherboard cottage was sitting at the top of the incline behind some shrubs. The back of the house would have stunning views of the hills. Then I saw Jev waiting for me outside, pointing to the top of the steep driveway. I was going to have to reverse down – there was no way I could reverse up it when I left. As I slowly made my way down, two knocks on my rear window from Jev told me to stop.

I carefully stepped out of the car, which was on an incline, and saw again those long legs moving towards me. 'Hello,' he said. 'How was the drive?'

'Siri made it easy, and very little traffic.'

He leaned towards me and gave me a hug. 'I'm glad to hear that. But it's still early, traffic usually builds around lunchtime. It's the wineries around here, they're very popular on weekends.'

He then led the way down some steps to his house, steep steps with no handrail. I was glad that I'd opted for the boots. The first thing I noticed when we walked through the front door was the clutter, something I'd recently been assessing in my life. It was bright and clean, but almost every surface was covered with things – books, papers, pens, empty serving bowls, keys. And guitars lined the walls of the living room, even some sitting on stands. A musician's home, and one living alone.

Before moving into my new home, I had read Marie Kondo's book *The Life-Changing Magic of Tidying Up*. I found the process of de-cluttering my life a liberating one, from my marriage to my possessions. And it seemed to open up room for new possibilities – well, that was the idea behind it, and it did feel that way. The possibility for new beginnings to come into the cleared space. All obstacles removed.

The weather was mild and he suggested we have a cup of tea out on the deck. I followed him into the kitchen where he put the kettle on the stove and grabbed some blue willow teacups from an overhead cupboard. I looked around the room and noticed more clutter. The benchtops were covered with things that might have been put away in a cupboard or drawer; a juicer, a toaster, a marble mortar and pestle, a box of crackers, salt and pepper shakers, a sugar bowl, a butter dish, a knife, and more empty bowls. I had to resist the urge to start clearing things away.

With the teapot and cups on a tray we moved out onto the deck. The view really was breathtaking. He told me he'd built the deck himself and it was clear that he was proud of the result. Everything was so green and still, and the sky felt just a little closer. There was a huge sequoia at the bottom of his backyard, as well as an oak tree. And so many birds – magpies, currawongs, rosellas, cockatoos.

We talked about our marriages, their beginnings and their endings. He told me that after his divorce he went through a period of depression that lasted a while. Then he decided to start doing something about it: self-development courses – spiritual and physical – and some counselling. And then he started dating. He told me more about his experiences on RSVP, the series of casual encounters after his first post-divorce relationship of one year ended. I was curious to know more about that first relationship, why and how it ended, but I didn't want to appear nosy. It wasn't what he wanted, the casual encounters that followed, but that's what came his way. A younger male colleague at school had suggested he simply enjoy it while it lasted. He had once dated several women at the same time, none of them knew, but he really didn't think it would have bothered them. Everyone seemed to be satisfied with the way things were.

Jev told me that he was becoming a little disillusioned and seriously considered adopting a similar attitude as his colleague, something he'd never thought of before, not even in his younger days as a muso in New Zealand. But still, he hesitated.

'And then you met me, right?' I said, smiling.

'Yeah, you're right.' He smiled, that very small smile, then asked, 'What do you want?'

A very direct question. I suddenly felt like I was at a job interview, but I wasn't taken aback by the question, or it's suddenness. I didn't have to stop and think about my reply. I knew what I wanted, and I told him. 'I want to rediscover the person I used to be, pre-marriage. I want to reconnect with her.'

He looked surprised. 'Not many people can answer that question so easily.'

'Really? Who have you asked?'

'Some of the women I've dated. They weren't sure, they couldn't give me an answer right away. Some said they hadn't really thought about it. I soon realised that says a lot.'

'Is that your test question then? And women either pass or fail?'

'Yeah, I suppose you could see it that way. You could say it's just the teacher in me.' He smiled again and reached across and put his hand over mine. 'What do you think, shall we go inside and get lunch going?'

I looked at my watch, it was almost 1:00. Where had the time gone?

He had everything ready to go, and I didn't have to do a thing. Something I wasn't used to.

He moved around the kitchen with what I can only call grace, a sort of gliding, no clumsiness. He knew his way around and every movement flowed, from reaching for a hanging pot to slicing vegetables with a knife, all like a choreographed performance. Lamb chops, parsnip, carrots and seasoning, all in the pan and then into the oven.

I couldn't remember the last time a man prepared a meal for me. Only in Italy, and that had been over thirty years ago. He was like a memory, a fond memory.

An Interrupted Life

We had lunch on the deck. I commented on how good it was and he seemed pleased. He'd offered me wine but I don't usually drink in the middle of the day so we had mineral water instead. Sitting on the deck was the most relaxed I'd been in a long time. It felt so peaceful, I could have stayed put, but he reminded me that I had a haircut appointment. How could I have forgotten; I'd been thinking about it all week. But I didn't tell him that. We moved back inside and left the dishes in the sink – more important things awaited.

He had things all set up in the spare room, it could almost have passed for a hairdressing salon – the adjustable chair, a cape, a water spray bottle, scissors, a stool on wheels for him, and combs and clips all lined up on a small table. I sat down in front of the mirrored dressing table and he placed the cape around my shoulders, securing it tightly with the Velcro strips. He sat on the stool and started sectioning my hair, moving easily from side to side. Then with a comb in one hand and scissors in the other, he started carefully trimming the ends. I looked in the mirror and saw a man I barely knew cutting my hair, but he looked like he knew what he was doing. He was very focussed and he didn't talk, unlike my experiences with other hairdressers where all sorts of things were talked about, all sorts of things revealed. At one point I moved my hands out from under the cape and placed them on my lap. He stopped what he was doing and covered them up again. Then he resumed cutting my hair.

When he finished he picked up a mirror, just as a professional hairdresser would do, to show me the result. I nodded my approval. My hair was now sitting just above my shoulders with some layering at the front. No need to wear it up as I had been doing. I liked it.

'Thank you, that looks great. It's been a long time since my last visit to the hairdresser,' I said, smiling at him in the mirror.

He seemed pleased that I was a satisfied client, and I was. As I was about to get up, he leaned forward and put his arms around me. Then he started running his hands over the cape, up and down my arms and then across my breasts. Then he moved his hands under the cape and continued to stroke my breasts. He looked at me in the mirror and said, 'Would you like a lie down before you leave?'

If he wasn't still stroking my breasts, I would have thought he was actually suggesting a rest. But I knew what he meant. 'That sounds like a good idea.'

He took off the cape, took my hand, and lead me to the bedroom.

I didn't feel uncomfortable or anxious, and I wasn't thinking about how things would proceed. He stopped and looked at me, his face inches away from mine and his arms hanging over my shoulders.

'I have to tell you that I've been thinking about you, and about this moment, the entire week. The moment I saw you step out of the car this morning I got an erection. I'm not sure if it's the same feeling for you, but I want to fuck you, slowly and for a long time.'

What could I say? I put my arms around his waist and stretched up to kiss him, a long, slow kiss. A kiss that I hoped would say more than words. This wasn't the first *RSVP* hook-up for him, but it was for me. First post-divorce sex with an unknown man, and on the second date. That really was the pre-marriage me. I was on the right path to rediscovering her.

He started to undress and I did the same. I admired his lean body and long legs, and his feet, long and slender like his hands. As odd as it sounds, the word that came to my mind was 'intelligent' – they were intelligent-looking feet. Then my gaze travelled up his legs and I noticed his erection protruding from his boxer shorts. His body was that of a younger man's, there wasn't any mid-life flab in sight. I wasn't shy about taking off my clothes and standing naked in front of Jev. I was too full of anticipation to be thinking about it, and the older me had left behind anxieties about not having perfectly even breasts or the size and shape of things. Yes, age had helped me let those insecurities go. And then there had been *RSVP* Mark looking at my body, the up and down perusal, as I moved around. At the time I didn't stop to think about it, I didn't know he was checking me out. It was only after his, 'You're that rare thing, someone I fancy' message that I understood what he was doing. He was imagining me naked, and liking what he saw. That helped my self-confidence.

Jev lit some candles on the bedside table while I got into bed and waited for him to join me. He turned and stood at the edge of the bed looking at me, a smile on his face. He seemed to be anticipating what was to come and savouring every moment. I pulled the bedsheet back, inviting him to get in. And he did. He moved towards me and once again I had that feeling of familiarity. I knew his body. I knew his touch. Somehow, I knew. We spent the afternoon making love. At one point he asked me to tell him what I liked. I was taken aback; I'd never been asked that before. It seemed a little too clinical to have to put in words what I wanted him to do, a bit like providing an instruction manual. So instead, I took his hand and showed him. His hands travelled around my body in just the right way. He wasn't in a hurry and I was fully present, unlike the latter years of my marriage where sex had become more routine and I sometimes was somewhere else, and with someone else, in my mind. First-time sex is more often than not clumsy and awkward, but it wasn't with Jev. It was good, so good, right from the beginning. Everything felt right. There wasn't a thing I would have changed.

It really had been a perfect day and I left feeling as though this might well be the beginning of a new life for me. I had a new hairdresser, and a new lover in one. Maybe I'd hit the jackpot.

Chapter 7

My new life post-divorce had got off to a good start and I was excited about what was to come. We made plans to see each other again the following Saturday in Healesville, and I would be bringing lunch. Jev wanted to take me on a tour of the township and go on a real forest walk, something I was looking forward to. I spent the week thinking about it, and him. Apart from a couple of days of teaching, I was free to do a lot of thinking, and I felt free.

I arrived just after 10:00 on the Saturday morning. I knocked but there was no answer. I opened the front door which was unlocked, always unlocked, and called his name. No response. I put my backpack and basket of goodies down and walked to the back door and again called out. No response. I went back in the house, feeling uncomfortable that I had let myself in. As I walked towards the front door, I saw him appear suddenly on the veranda. I liked the way he moved; he seemed to be the sort of person who was never in a hurry.

There was a hug hello and we unpacked the basket of food. He commented on the basket, it was deep and round and a green colour he liked. I told him it was a gift from a one-time neighbour – a stolen gift.

'You're going to have to follow that with an explanation,' he said, looking amused.

'Well, he was walking in Clifton Hill one morning and saw a stand outside a shop with straw baskets hanging from it. He helped himself to one and walked away. I don't think he thought he was stealing; he simply took it as if he were reaching up to a tree branch to pick the fruit that was on offer. The stand, like a tree, was offering its fruit. He was always a bit odd.'

'And you kept the basket?' Again, a look of amusement on his face.

'I did consider returning it; I knew where the shop was. But it was a gift, sort of.'

'That's one way of looking at it. And it's a great basket, I think I would have done the same.'

An example of like-minded thinking? I thought so.

He suggested having a cup of tea out on the deck. It was mid-morning and it was sunny, perfect weather to be outside, and then there was the view of rolling hills, spectacular. He put two cups and a pot of tea – real tea, not teabags – on a tray and led the way outside onto the deck. Then he went back inside to grab one of his guitars. I got the feeling that wherever he went, his guitar went with him. Like an extension of himself.

We sat in the sunshine and talked. For almost two hours. We talked about the working week; he had anecdotes about staff members and students, and his methods of managing both. He was funny and he made me laugh. I talked about my days in different schools, some good some bad, but it was always good to be able to leave as soon as the bell went at the end of the day. No after school meetings to attend. We agreed on that, too. We talked more about our marriages and what went wrong and about our other significant relationships. I asked a lot of questions, which I have a tendency to do, and he was very forthcoming with his answers. Unlike some people, he didn't think it was a taboo subject.

And then I asked him the question he had asked me on our first meeting.

'What do you want?' I told him I was asking because there was a Part B to my answer.

He stopped to think. 'What I'd eventually like to do is work less. I've been teaching for over thirty years. And it's not that I haven't enjoyed being in the classroom, I just think now that I don't have any dependents, or a mortgage to pay off, there's the possibility to do other things.'

'Any idea what those other things might be?'

He turned his gaze to the hills, but he didn't have a ready answer, or an answer he was willing to share. Instead, he asked, 'So, what's your Part B?'

'I'll be right back.' I went inside to get my copy of Jack Gilbert's collected poems from my backpack. When I went back out he was playing his guitar, but I could see that he was a little intrigued. He sat looking at me, still gently strumming his guitar, as I opened the book at page 192 and read the poem *I Imagine The Gods* aloud, the whole poem with emphasis on the last verse. I didn't follow my reading with an explanation, I didn't think I needed to. And he didn't ask me to; he just looked at me while still playing his guitar, like an accompaniment to the poem.

But that was what I wanted, what the poem says, to be fully alive in my life, and to fall in love one last time. After sitting in post-poetry reading silence for a few minutes, I asked him if he'd experienced love since his divorce nine years ago. I was thinking of the woman he'd had the year-long relationship with.

'No, but fondness, yes.'

'Fondness?'

'Yeah, I was fond of her. She was my first relationship after the divorce, and I had been single for five years. So, it was a pretty important relationship, what they call the 'transitional relationship'. We had some good times together.'

It made me stop and think about the word. To feel fondness for someone was to feel affection, to care, but not to love, not to be *in* love. Fondness, it's a word that floats lightly, it carries no weight. But did he want to love deeply again, as he had his wife? He didn't say, and I didn't ask.

I watched as he continued playing a riff and I could see by the expression on his face that with a guitar in his hands he was perfectly at home; his real home. He was looking across at the view and he seemed for those few moments to be at one with everything around him. He was lost in another world. I sat and watched, almost envious that he could experience such a state. And I was almost afraid to speak, to break the spell, but it was time for lunch and I was aware that I would need to get going soon after that.

The meat stew I had bought just needed to be warmed up, it didn't take long. He cooked some rice to go with it in his pressure cooker, which was also ready in a matter of minutes. Watching him reach for utensils and open cupboards and pick up plates and stir the stew ... it was all so seductive. He seemed to enjoy being in the kitchen, and that too was seductive. I'm not sure why that stood out for me, maybe it was because my ex was never the one in the kitchen during our marriage. Watching Jev, in whatever room he was in, I realised that I'd never felt quite so drawn to someone physically. I'd never felt quite so at ease. And I didn't have to try and present my best self. I wasn't uncomfortable being myself.

We went back outside and had lunch on the deck, there really was no better place to be. He enjoyed the stew, which was one of my mother's recipes, a traditional Italian dish. We talked about food and cooking and shared favourite recipes. He suggested taking me out to dinner one night at the Grand Hotel in town, which also had live bands playing. I couldn't remember the last time I'd been to a live performance, and there was a reason. I didn't feel comfortable in noisy environments, crowded noisy environments in particular. But I didn't do what I usually do – appear interested but secretly plan how I could avoid going; a sudden illness, a friend in need, a flat battery. Over time I had collected a few reliable excuses. I just told him that going to see live bands wasn't really my thing. He didn't seem surprised or disappointed, which surprised me as he was someone who used to perform live, and who enjoyed going out.

He'd told me about some of the things he did with the woman he dated for a year. They went on holiday to New

Zealand together, and had a city getaway staying in a hotel and exploring the Melbourne nightlife, and attended a rock concert, and went scuba diving, and went out for dinner regularly. He asked me what I *did* enjoy doing. Again, I didn't stop to think. I was completely open and told him that I enjoyed walks in nature and visiting a gallery or museum and small gatherings, preferably for lunch, and sometimes going to cafes with outdoor seating and cosy evenings at home with a book and the cat on my lap. He smiled and said, 'Little adventures. We can do those together.'

I fell in love with him right then and there. Here was a man who didn't judge me. Who accepted my quirks and was willing to accommodate them. I felt a flush of relief, and joy. I wasn't going to have to subject myself to activities that I didn't enjoy. I wasn't going to have to pretend and endure. I had done enough of that in my marriage.

A wind had picked up so we decided to postpone our walk for another time. He didn't like walking in the forest when it was windy, he didn't think it was safe. In the time that he'd lived in Healesville there had been several instances of branches and trees falling and causing serious injuries, even death, to walkers. That, and he had other plans for the afternoon. He reached across and took my bare arm in his hand, gently sliding his fingers up and down as if he was holding the neck of his guitar. It felt so good, I didn't want him to stop. We sat a while longer without talking. With words, that is.

Jev was a tender lover and a generous one. It wasn't about his pleasure; he wanted to please. And I'm sure that in itself gave him pleasure, or something else. He worked his way around my body with an amazing ease and understanding, he knew when to change his rhythm to match mine. We were never out of sync. I could see him watching me carefully, a smile appearing on his face when he sensed my enjoyment. And he knew what to say, his words weren't a distraction; they were about me, about us, and they added to my pleasure. Sometimes he waited until the very end; on one occasion he whispered, 'I adore you. You're magnificent.' The expression on his face was one of utter joy. Our bodies moved together with a knowingness I couldn't quite understand. When we were in bed together, we knew each other, completely. Afterwards, lying with our arms and legs entwined, we were as if one body. I hadn't felt so comfortable, so at one, lying naked with a man in a long time.

Jev told me there was something he discovered about himself after his divorce; it was during his later encounters. He discovered that he was a sexual being. At the time I didn't think too much about it. I knew that he'd been celibate for a long time after his divorce and it was only natural that he missed having sex, and then enjoyed rediscovering it. It was only later that I fully understood what he meant.

Chapter 8

And so a routine was being established, of alternating weekend visits between Healesville and Fairfield. I thought it was the ideal situation; we got to enjoy country and city living, and he thought so too. The following weekend we spent at my place, and it involved an overnight stay. He would be arriving Saturday morning and leaving Sunday afternoon. I was a little nervous about the sleeping over thing. That would involve sharing space and personal habits in a more intimate way – the sleep habits, the bathroom habits, and the first thing in the morning habits. Things that in a marriage become ordinary. But with Jev I lost my inhibitions quickly, I became less self-conscious and a little more relaxed. Maybe because he was so uninhibited himself. He was comfortable walking around naked and showering with the bathroom door open. But then, he was easy to look at.

An Interrupted Life

Sitting at my computer near the front window I could see when his car came up the driveway. As he pulled up outside my window, I sat and watched as he got out of the car. It always put a smile on my face to see what he was wearing; he enjoyed dressing well, and he had a sense of style. He liked hats, and he looked good wearing one. He often complimented me on my fashion choices. And I liked that he noticed.

After he arrived and unloaded his things, his overnight bag and his guitar – always the guitar – we had a cup of tea and then went for a walk along Station Street, a street that offered a variety of shops and restaurants and cafes. It was a Saturday morning and there were a lot of people about. I noticed that he drew attention as we walked along the footpath; he cut a striking figure in his black jeans, tight-fitting knit jumper and grey Stetson.

But it was more than that.

It was the way his arms moved, the way his legs took long strides along the footpath, the way his footsteps landed lightly on the ground. But he didn't seem to notice the glances, mostly from women. He was oblivious. Instead, he noticed colours and shapes and objects. One time someone had left a piece of rusty metal on the nature strip. He immediately stopped to look and take a photo. He later transformed the image into an abstract painting. Where I saw a piece of garbage, he saw a work of art.

We visited the Manchester shop, and the op shop, and then we stopped at a rug shop. Jev noticed what looked like a small guitar in the window and right away he took an interest. He suggested we go inside and wander around. We admired a few of the rugs, expensive rugs, and when the young salesman approached, Jev asked him what the instrument in the window was. The expression on the salesman's face told me that he wasn't disappointed that we weren't inquiring about a rug; he immediately explained that it was a Turkish saz and then he showed us a larger one that was sitting behind the counter. They started a discussion about the strings and the shape and the sound. That's when the salesman sat down on a nearby stool and started playing it.

It was a beautiful sound – soulful, melancholy – and we both stood there transfixed. After he finished playing, we continued talking and he invited us to a celebration of Turkish music at the Immigration Museum later that day. A customer arrived and asked about a rug in the window and the salesman seemed almost annoyed by the interruption. He would much rather have continued talking to Jev.

When we left, we decided to do a shop at the supermarket across the road and get some supplies for dinner. We stood at the kerb waiting for a break in the traffic; we were going to have to make a dash and stop in the middle of the road and stand there until it was safe to cross to the other side. I remember that I hesitated and suggested that we walk back down the street to the traffic lights. He didn't say anything, he simply reached down and took my hand and guided me across the road, his body like a shield against the cars whizzing by. My little adventure for the day, crossing a busy road. But I could have been anywhere, doing anything. With Jev, I felt safe.

We spent the rest of the weekend going for walks, playing scrabble, cooking, and listening to music, his music. He had recordings of songs he had written in 2007 when he was part of a duo called The Honey Eaters. One of the songs became part of the soundtrack for Sarah Watt's feature film, *My Year Without Sex*. I loved the song, 'Upset Girl'. He gave me the CD and I played it over and over again. It was beautiful, the lyrics and the music. And I liked the sound of his voice, it had a reverberating quality that was very sensuous. It was clear that he had talent.

After listening to the CD, I knew he really was first and foremost a musician. I couldn't help but wonder what might have been if he hadn't come to Australia with his then-wife. If he hadn't taken on a mortgage and had children. If he hadn't had to take a regular job because of those commitments. I suppose the 'what ifs' that exist in all our lives.

We had just finished an early dinner on the Sunday night, and, after a busy, fun-filled day, we were feeling a little tired. We both thought it would be a good idea to have a rest before he drove back to Healesville. We lay on the bed chatting and laughing. At one point he raised himself on his elbow and looked at me, then he leaned in and kissed me. A gentle kiss. I smiled. He stopped and looked at me as if he was considering something, and then he leapt off the bed and started undressing. 'That's it. I'm not going anywhere when you look at me like that. I can't leave now.'

And so, he stayed for another hour and we made love again. The third time that day.

After he left, I went back to bed and I felt his absence, a palpable absence. I lay there thinking about him, and waiting for his text telling me that he'd arrived home safely. I thought about the way he sometimes talked to me when we were making love. It was like words on a page; it felt like I was listening to a story, a story about us.

The night before, while we were lying in bed, we'd been talking about work and how sometimes we stay in a job we don't really like, something we had both experienced, and how we tolerate circumstances that we know we're not really happy with. It's change that we resist, in our working life and our personal life. He realised after his divorce that although he didn't want to part ways, he wasn't really happy in his marriage either. And it wasn't just her dissatisfaction that changed their relationship, he realised that they were very different people.

Again, something I could relate to.

I tolerated so much in my marriage without even realising it. It really was after an experience I wasn't expecting that I saw the life I was living as if for the first time. As a friend put it, it was a necessary experience; the catalyst that opened my eyes and made me recognise the need for change. But that's another story.

Later, as we were drifting off to sleep, I heard him say, 'It's only circumstances, and circumstances change.' I didn't ask him what he meant. We both fell asleep soon after, his arms wrapped tightly around me. But I remembered the words, and they stayed with me.

His text arrived as soon as he got back to Healesville:

[J] Home now. A brilliant weekend xx

Yes, it really had been.

The more time we spent together the more I realised that he emanated a stillness and strength that I hadn't come across before. And that was exactly what I needed, someone with a calm nature that counterbalanced my neuroses, like a calming blanket. He didn't get flustered or impatient, and he didn't expect me to be other than what I was. I felt accepted. And he had a physical strength too, he seemed to have boundless energy. The word indefatigable fitted him perfectly.

Chapter 9

When I told my friends about my *RSVP* experiences they were amused. When I told them that I was seeing Jev they were curious. The, 'How are things?' question that was really asking for more details of my new relationship. What was life like after leaving a long-term marriage? What was dating at an older age really like? And maybe more specifically, what was the sex like?

I had a semi-regular catch up with two women from my old neighbourhood, Anna and Lucy. Anna had divorced when her two children were eight and ten years old, and at the age of sixty-three hadn't had a long-term relationship since. She'd been living alone for years. Lucy was a little younger and lived with her husband and adult son.

I remember Anna, who didn't hold back when giving her opinion, quizzing me about how often Jev and I saw each other, and how we spent our time together. I told her that we spent weekends together and most of the school holidays too.

I told her about our regular weekend outings in the city and forest walks in the country and other fun things.

'Fun things.'

That was her brief response, her way of summing up our relationship in two words. But with an emphasis that told me that she had more to say. Lucy sat back with a smile on her face, a smile she was trying hard to repress, waiting for what she knew was coming. A brief reply was not Anna's style. Maybe it was her own past experiences of failed relationships that compelled her to give advice, all the time. She did have that as a sort of expertise.

'You're in a relationship with someone that you mostly see on weekends. So, really, you're having a weekend relationship, and that probably suits you both but you can't say it's the same as a committed relationship with all the ups and downs that come with it. I don't think you can really know someone when you don't have to deal with the challenges of life together, even just the everyday ones. How can you know if you really get along if it's all just fun? What happens if there's a problem, even just an everyday domestic problem? You're not there to deal with it together. You're not there to help each other when there's a need, big or small. It's a bit like permanent dating, and some people do prefer that. That's perfectly understandable. But it's not the same as a committed relationship.'

She certainly didn't hold back. I could see Lucy looking at us, trying to contain her amusement. I tried a small attempt to make her understand. 'I don't think a relationship is about frequency, it's about quality. We talk every day, and send messages during the day, and there's always a call at night and sometimes first thing in the morning. We only live an hour apart, it's not that far. I guess it's early days too.'

'So, you think you might make the decision to live together one day down the track? And how would that work? Who would move? Would you leave your community and friends and son to live in Healesville?'

I didn't want to debate the pros and cons of my relationship with Jev, or discuss our plans for the future. It didn't feel right. We were still in the early stage of our relationship, the so-called honeymoon phase, where we were high on dopamine. We were caught up in the newness of it, and yes, it was fun. We weren't ready to make any decisions about cohabiting. We were having lots of little adventures and lots of passionate sex. We were happy. But I couldn't tell Anna that. I tried one last attempt to help her understand.

'Jev makes me feel safe. He's like an anchor in my life after the turbulence of divorce, and I like that.'

She smiled. 'Yes, and an anchor can sink a ship.' Her ready reply told me she wasn't going to be convinced.

'As I said, it's early days. Anything can happen.'

I think she got the message, and I didn't want to continue talking about it.

Regular street parties were a thing in my old neighbourhood and there was always plenty of good food, music, and company. It was a way of catching up with neighbours, some of whom had also become friends. The first one after I'd moved away from the neighbourhood was coming up, and both Jev and I were invited. Jev was keen to go and meet some of my friends and so we did.

I remember seeing faces I hadn't seen in a while, some of them staring at me with surprise. One woman approached me and said, 'You look beautiful, and so happy,' and then proceeded to look me up and down. And another, 'You're looking amazing. I love the jacket.'

I couldn't quite understand their reactions – had I really changed so much? There I was in a new leather jacket, bought on one of our visits to the op shop, tight black pants tucked into brown knee-high boots – also a purchase from the op shop – and with a new haircut. Yes, I had changed. I was nothing like the woman I used to be. And standing next to me was Jev in his black leather jacket and black Stetson, my new partner.

I was happy. That's what they saw.

Chapter 10

I used to keep a journal when I was younger, and after I met Jev I started again. So much had changed in my life and I wanted to write about it. It helped. I wanted to be able to navigate this new period in my life with a little more awareness than I had done in my marriage. I wanted to be more present, more in tune with my feelings, more reflective. I didn't want to make the same mistakes.

When I told Jev I was doing this, in the spirit of open communication, he frowned and said, 'You might be overthinking things. You don't need to analyse our relationship, and we don't need to talk about what's making it work. It's good and it's working and we're moving closer together. We have a connection, a deep one. We both can feel that.'

I wasn't sure what to say. I didn't try to explain, or try and get him to understand, I didn't want to be preaching a message he didn't want to hear. It was only later that I remembered that his wife had also kept a journal, a journal to record how she was feeling during their marriage. That might have been the reason for his lack of enthusiasm when I mentioned my idea. But he didn't say.

He'd done a Vipassana meditation course after his marriage ended. It was a technique that involved observing thoughts and feelings but not dwelling on them, and not analysing them. Jev would sometimes say, 'We can't believe everything we think, that only makes us prisoners of our thoughts,' as if they were the source of our suffering. But I'm a thinker and like talking about things in order to better understand them. I like the clarity that words can bring. He thought that intellectualising our feelings was part of the overthinking problem. His was an 'it is what it is' attitude to life. And so, I wrote about it in my journal instead, and that got me thinking even more.

> *Jev said I 'overthink' things? Do I? I tried to initiate a conversation with him about the importance of communication in a relationship, but it didn't go far. Not sure why. I would have thought that after the end of his marriage he might think otherwise …*

I started reading articles about what makes a successful relationship, what the characteristics are, the secrets and tips for a happy and healthy one, how to develop and strengthen it. Most of them referred to ongoing communication through an open exchange of personal feelings. I sent a few of the articles – maybe too many – to Jev, wanting to share them with him, and to make him aware of how I was feeling; that I wanted for us to keep the dialogue going and to feel that we could talk openly about anything. And maybe I was using the articles as evidence of just how important it was. I don't think he read them. I saw that he received them on Messenger but I didn't get a response, and he didn't mention them. Instead, he sent me some photos he'd taken on one of his nature walks. I sent back a comment, I always did. I didn't give it too much thought; yes, that was a challenge, but I decided not to be so obsessive. To be a little more relaxed, a more go with the flow attitude. His more Zen way of being in the world.

After we'd known each other for just over a year Jev was asked to go away on a school camp to Central Australia. He was going to be on the camp for a week but we wouldn't be seeing each other for two weeks; he'd be going straight back to work afterwards and it wouldn't be until the following weekend that we'd be able to see each other. It was the first time we would be apart for so long, and with very little phone contact due to reception problems in the outback.

As a teacher, I knew that camps are part of the school curriculum and part of a teacher's responsibilities, but I felt a little annoyed that he hadn't talked to me about it before accepting, that he hadn't expressed some reluctance about going because he would be away from me for longer than usual. I was annoyed that he was looking forward to the trip, that he was excited about going. Perhaps it was a little irrational of me, but I wanted him to not want to go, I wanted him to tell me that he couldn't get out of it, I wanted him to tell me that he'd miss me. But he didn't.

We saw each other on the Friday night; he came after school and left early the next morning. Instead of watching his car come up the driveway, I stood and watched as it went the other way. He was leaving and all I could think was that he was leaving me. It was Saturday morning and I found myself alone for the first time in a long time with the weekend ahead and no plans. It was the first time in all the time that I'd been living in my new home that I felt alone. When I walked back in the house, I sensed a new emptiness. I missed him, even though he'd just left, and I didn't like that I did. I didn't like that I felt lost on my own, in my own home. I was surprised, and a little annoyed that at my age I would be feeling this way. After all, I'd left a long-term marriage to be on my own. I should be able to be alone.

I didn't hear from him for a few days, no good morning messages and no good night calls. I felt his absence as a physical pain. How quickly I had become accustomed to the presence of another person in my life, how quickly I had become accustomed to hearing his voice, even if on the phone, every day. How quickly I had allowed another person to be the source of my joy. Yes, we had a connection, but I seemed to have grown too dependent on his company, his presence in my life. I'd noticed that if for some reason he didn't call at his usual time I would begin to wonder why. Morning texts, evening messages, they had become our routine, a daily routine, just as getting up and having breakfast and then dinner at the end of the day with someone you lived with would be. If that person didn't appear to either of those, it would be natural to worry, to be alarmed, and to try and find out why. That's how I responded to missed calls or messages: 'Where are you?' 'Did you get my message?' 'You might be on the phone.' I worried.

After four days of not hearing from him, he finally did call, but it was a brief conversation and there was a tone in his voice that I wasn't expecting. It was almost joyous. He was in the outback, free and happy and having fun.

He posted pictures on his Facebook page with comments – that's how I got the updates. There were photos of him standing with students on either side of him and his arms draped over their shoulders, Uluru and the Olgas in the background. They were all wearing bright green T-shirts with an image of the rock, and they were all looking very happy. The caption read: 'On Year 10 camp in Central Australia. The kids are fantastic and my fellow staffers, magnificent. Many highlight moments and we get to sleep under the stars every night, and one night underground in Coober Pedy. The Australian Outback is pure magic!'

It suddenly dawned on me that being a teacher, a respected teacher, was a huge part of his identity. He was Mr T. What would he be without that? Could he give that up? He talked about retiring and pursuing his music and art, but I wasn't sure it would be so easy. And he didn't seem to be missing me. That continued to bother me.

But what bothered me more was that I felt that way. Was I that insecure? As teachers we'd had conversations about differentiation in the classroom, the need to tailor a lesson to meet individual needs, and how that was sometimes a challenge. I realised that there was another place for differentiation that was also challenging, and that was in a relationship; the ability to maintain a sense of autonomy while being in a close and intimate relationship. He'd talked about emotionally needy women he'd met, and suddenly it crossed my mind that was how he would be interpreting my 'I miss you' messages. Yes, I sent a few.

He did the differentiation thing better than I did. The Jev on camp, I felt as though I didn't know him. All the talk about moving closer together, about connection, where was that? I got a few brief responses to my messages but I felt as though I was annoying him, that my messages were becoming tiresome. Yes, there were also a couple of, 'Do you miss me?' texts after his lack of response to mine, but I wanted to know, I *needed* to know.

One thing I could do during our time apart was to stop and reflect on how things were going, to think about the relationship and if it was meeting my needs. I took the opportunity of my grumpy mood to reflect on things that were beginning to annoy me. His sarcasm was one. There sometimes was a bit of derision in his humour. Some might call it a quirky sense of humour, but I thought there was a hint of mockery. I had an old cat and I was a bit concerned that he'd spend most of the day curled up sleeping; sometimes

I'd have to nudge him awake at meal times. Jev had had cats in the past and I once asked him if he thought it was unusual that my cat was sleeping more than usual. His response? 'That's what all cats do. He's not going to get up and play the guitar.' I did think that lacked sensitivity, and I tried to tell him, but he became defensive. I was 'overreacting'.

And then there were the photos. I noticed that he would take a lot of photos of me, of us. Some he posted on his Facebook page. I didn't do the posting thing; I didn't like putting my life on show. He once told me that he showed a colleague at work a photo of me. Her reaction was, 'No way is she fifty-eight.'

That annoyed me even more because he seemed to be putting me on display, like 'look who I'm dating'. More of an ego thing, I thought. Then I remembered his comment when I hovered around him in the kitchen making suggestions like, 'Do you think maybe you should add more water to the soup?', which I would secretly do when he moved away. Or, 'I'm not sure about putting raisins in the ragu sauce.'

He was a cook who liked to improvise, whereas I followed recipes – traditional ones, in particular. That's when he made the comment that I had a tendency to micromanage; that I was micromanaging him in the kitchen. Well, maybe I had high standards, or used to have.

And it wasn't the same as controlling, which I gently pointed out. I also reminded him that he once thanked me for reminding him to contact his other son, the one who lived overseas. They had very sporadic contact, but after sending messages prompted by me, they maintained more regular communication, even phone calls. He had actually said,

'That's why you're good for me.' And then suddenly I became a micromanager?

When we walked at the parklands he preferred staying on the path and walking towards the industrial zone. I liked to walk off the path and through the trees. It was under one of those trees that we sat and had our first encounter. He liked taking photos along the way – of graffiti on the buildings and the bridges, which he then used to create his art – and of other things. There was a sign reminding people to keep their dogs on a lead, but the figure of the person didn't have any feet; the legs ended in stumps at the ankles. Jev found that particularly amusing and took a photo and sent it to his colleague at work who shared a similar sense of humour. Not sure what his message said, but no doubt it was in keeping with his quirky humour.

And then there was Scrabble. He was very competitive and wasn't satisfied until he reached a score of three hundred, and he had to win. Even if I got tired, or simply had had enough, he wanted to keep playing. In order to end the game sooner I had to resort to cheating. I would sneak extra letters without him noticing, which wasn't hard to do because he was too focussed on his tiles and trying to get a high score. Then I would form a word using all my letters, get fifty bonus points and the points from his unused letters, and win the game. He didn't like to lose and would remain in a glum mood afterwards. Yes, that was annoying and tiresome, but I was always secretly amused. I had to disappear quickly to another room and have a private giggle. I sometimes wondered what his reaction would have been if he knew I'd been cheating. Not a good one, I was sure.

They say that time apart for couples can be a time to recharge and a time to reflect, on the good and not so good. I had done that, and discovered that sometimes Jev annoyed me. But still, I missed him.

Chapter 11

When he got back, we got back to the usual routine. He arrived on a Saturday morning, and seeing him again was like seeing him for the first time. I was full of excitement and anticipation as I watched his Toyota Corolla come up the driveway. He was taking the Monday off work and he would be staying over for three days then heading off to work early on the Tuesday morning. Apart from some shopping and cooking and walks at the parklands, we spent most of the time at home. Lots of talking and listening to music and making love, and some Scrabble too. We didn't socialise much, apart from a conversation or two with my neighbour, who lived in the townhouse behind me; most of the time it was just the two of us.

We did have one outing on the Sunday, lunch at an Italian restaurant in Thornbury. We sat in the courtyard out the back, which had vines growing along the neighbouring brick walls and flowers growing in pots; it was like sitting in a garden. We were quietly sipping a glass of prosecco while we waited for our meals to arrive; I chose the antipasto dish and he decided on the eggplant parmigiana. He put his glass down and looked at me. 'What are you thinking?'

'Just thinking how good it is to see you again.'

'Yeah, me too.'

'Yes, but did you miss me while you were away?' My raised eyebrows and the smile on my face told him I wasn't being serious. There was no reprimand.

'Let me see. Between trekking across the outback in sweltering heat and travelling with a busload of rowdy students and sleeping in a tent with a snoring colleague and chasing a thief who was found going through our belongings, and making sure no one went missing, I can answer that with one word. Yes.'

I had to laugh; it wasn't what I was expecting, but it was typical Jev humour. And then he reached across and took my hand. 'And you know that.'

I didn't say anything, but I thought, *Well, I do now.*

After lunch he suggested a walk up the street, he'd never been in the area before and wanted to explore. I was reluctant because it looked like it was going to rain. He casually strolled back to the car to get an umbrella. And then we walked. It had been a while since I'd been there and it turned out to be another little adventure.

There was an independent cinema I didn't know about, and a vintage clothing shop that we stopped to check out, and a retro furniture shop, and a café with terrazzo floors, a billiard table, and an older Italian woman behind the counter. While he was hitting a few balls, I had a cup of tea and chatted to the woman in Italian, and some of the other customers who all happened to be older Italian men. Some of them flirted with me, as Italian men will do at any age. But I felt suddenly at home, and I didn't want to leave. And speaking Italian again, I didn't realise how much I'd missed it. Both my parents were dead and the only Italians I knew were a few who lived in my area. Sadly, the post-war immigrants were getting older, and dying.

On the way home, the word Jev used to describe the shopping strip was 'funky'. It really was, and fun.

I found my journal entry for that weekend:

> *Jev's back. And what a wonderful weekend it's been! Every day filled with something delightful. I was woken early, two-thirty am. He drew me closer to him and we went back to sleep, reluctantly. Then again at five-thirty, but this time it was a time for delights ... laughter, kisses, tenderness, touch, loving words, connection. This morning has been a magical time. And I don't feel tired. I feel light. Free. Happy.*

And then this:

> *When we were making love in the morning, I held him close and I felt the love of every man I've ever held. I felt grateful that he made me feel that, that I remembered the others. Whatever happens, I will never forget that moment. Never.*

It was a feeling that came over me suddenly. That had never happened before, to remember past lovers whilst with a current one. And it didn't feel inappropriate, at all. The entry ended on a funny note.

> *We went shopping for groceries this morning, he's going to make a beef and vegetable casserole for dinner tonight and I'm going to make pasta tomorrow. I needed eggs. Before putting the carton in the trolley, I opened it, as I usually do, to check that there were no broken ones. I noticed an earwig inside and I quickly closed the carton and put it in the trolley. I wanted to get it back outside where it belonged. It was only when we were loading the shopping into the car that Jev noticed. I took the carton to a nearby bush and released the earwig. He smiled. 'Do you think we should go back and check the other cartons?' Funny.*

Just a few months later Covid happened, and with it came a new way of living – living with a virus. But it was early days and there was still scepticism and doubt as to how serious the situation was, or might become. And there was still room for humour. Well, there was for Jev. There was lots of discussion at the time about the possible ways the virus might be transmitted, and Jev sent me something a spokesperson from the Department of Health had said:

> 'Even during sex, the main risk probably comes from being close face to face through droplet spread, through kissing and touching each other's faces. I am not aware of any evidence to date that the infection can be spread through vaginal intercourse per se.
> So please continue to wash your hands regularly and especially before sex.'

And then he ended the message with this:

[J] Be prepared, lots of handwashing coming up!

I wasn't sure which was more amusing: the spokesperson's advice or Jev's response.

Chapter 12

It was when we were lying in bed on the Monday afternoon that I noticed a change in his skin colour. It was a warm day and we were lying with just a sheet over us. As he turned to face me, I caught a glimpse of a yellow tinge across his shoulders and upper chest, it was the sunlight through the window that made it noticeable. I pointed it out to him, but looking down he couldn't see it, and he didn't seem to think it was anything unusual.

A few weeks went by and the yellow became a little more noticeable; it was even in the whites of his eyes. He said it was probably a mild flare up of his autoimmune condition PSC, and that it had happened before. It was caused by an increase in bilirubin, a fluid made by the liver, and it would subside on its own. He later told me that students at school had asked other teachers why Mr T was looking yellow. That's when I thought it was probably a good idea to see the doctor. He resisted the idea, and it was only after his school principal asked him about his health that he agreed to go. But he was busy doing other things and the appointment wasn't made; that, and he didn't have a GP that he saw regularly for check-ups. He didn't go to the doctor. He practised Qigong, a series of coordinated body movements, instead. He would get up in the morning and do a session followed by meditation, and again in the evening.

I was getting a little worried, and annoyed, at his indifference, and decided to find a local GP in his area who was taking new patients. I made an appointment for him to see Dr Gerald on a Saturday. And then I got searching on Google and what I read made me worry a little more.

Primary sclerosing cholangitis (PSC) was a condition that could take a long time to develop, but once it did it was usually a progressive illness with no cure, apart from a liver transplant. I remembered the conversation at the very beginning of our relationship, and I remembered hearing what he said but not realising the significance. I didn't stop to think. He was providing 'full disclosure', as a friend later put it, but I was too caught up in the newness of being single in my late-fifties and being on a date to understand that it required some sort of follow-up question. It's something he must have told the other women. Did they ask any questions? Did they ask about the prognosis? Did they go away and search Google for more information? Did what they discover make them reassess and reconsider? Was it the reason a few were only interested in a sexual relationship? Now I was really overthinking.

I went with him to the doctor's appointment. I wanted to be there to hear exactly what the doctor had to say, not Jev's take on it. As soon as the doctor saw Jev, he asked him how long he'd been experiencing jaundice. After hearing that he had PSC, he recommended a blood test as soon as possible, and a follow-up appointment once the results came through. There was a pathology clinic nearby, and he could go before school on Monday. It would only take a few minutes and the doctor would have the results the next day. But he didn't go. He kept forgetting and putting it off, and I had to keep reminding him and urging him.

But he didn't forget his sense of humour. He sent me an edited selfie he'd taken where his entire face was coloured a bright yellow, and he was smiling. Yes, it made me smile too. I didn't want to do the micromanaging thing, so on my last visit to his house I left a note attached to his fridge, next to his shopping list.

> *Remember to have the blood test tomorrow morning!*
> *The clinic opens at 8:00. GO!*

And finally, he did.

I knew what the doctor would be telling us, I knew what was causing the jaundice and why it was getting worse. The whites of his eyes were now almost completely yellow, and he started to experience itching at night, which interrupted his sleep. Dr Gerald looked at his screen and then recommended that Jev see a gastroenterologist as soon as possible. He told us that his bilirubin levels were very high, too high. The normal range was between three and twenty micromoles/litre; Jev's bilirubin was four hundred and nine micromoles/litre. He didn't say, but I knew what that meant – and so did Jev. His liver was beginning to fail.

The doctor wrote him a referral to Maroondah Hospital, which was only a thirty-minute drive away, and said he should make the appointment right away. He emphasised the importance of getting a proper assessment that would include scans of his liver. Instead, Jev booked an appointment to see his Chinese herbal medicine practitioner Warren, whom he had been to see when he first got his PSC diagnosis years ago. He came back from the appointment with some herbs and more Qigong movements to practice, morning and night. I wasn't against the idea of alternative treatments, but we needed a diagnosis first. Even Warren said he needed to know exactly what was going on. Yes, he looked at Jev's tongue and checked his pulse, but that wasn't the same as having a scan, which is what he needed.

At the time, I didn't think it was anything other than Jev wanting a more natural approach to treating his condition, but later I realised that he was in denial. He didn't want to face the prospect of a liver transplant, which Warren referred to as 'barbaric'. Jev didn't say, but it was clear that he agreed. He trusted Warren, and believed that he got him this far with his alternative treatments and that he could get him through the next stage of the journey as well, the more difficult stage. If that's what he wanted, I couldn't change his mind. I had to respect his decision.

What I did do was find a little more support from other alternative practitioners. I found an autoimmune wellness site that explored treatment through diet. It also had a few stories of recovery through dietary changes, mostly a Paleo diet, and one of the stories of recovery was of a man diagnosed with PSC. He was told by his doctors, as Jev had been, that the only treatment was a liver transplant, and that making dietary changes was a waste of time. He decided, much like Jev, that he wasn't going to sit and wait for his liver to fail, he was going to do everything that he could to heal himself. And it worked. He did it all through diet – an elimination diet and a restrictive one. I sent the link to Jev with a message:

> [I] This makes me think that a change in diet and other natural methods could be a good option. It's worth putting in a bit of effort and then evaluating the results.
>
> See what you think.

He was encouraged, we both were. He ordered the cookbook, keen to give it a go. I thought it was the right moment to get him to address his clutter problem, so I sent another link about the health benefits of decluttering your home. It was based on a Feng Shui approach, something that related to his Qigong practice; they both involved balancing energy known as *chi*, which was vital for good physical and mental health. It was a fairly long article, going into the energy in each room of the house, but the message was simple: you have to get rid of clutter, it drains energy. His response:

[J] This chat space is getting cluttered!

I had to smile. His humour, as usual, was right on target.

Suddenly, grocery shopping wasn't as much fun as it used to be. We stopped to read the ingredients on the packaging of every item, and most of them went back on the shelf. In order to follow the diet properly he had to prepare all his own meals; there was no opening a box of cereal, or a packet of crackers, or a tub of yoghurt, or a packet of pasta. He had to buy only fresh foods – lean meats, fish, vegetables, fruit and nuts and seeds. That was it; no dairy, no legumes, no grains, no processed food. Breakfast was an effort for him, as it had to be a cooked meal – mostly eggs and vegetables – and on a work day it was a bit of a challenge. To save time, he got into the habit of cooking an extra-large dinner and having the leftovers for breakfast, and sometimes lunch at work. But there were some tasty recipes, such as the basil pesto chicken with roasted vegetables that became one of his favourites.

The website said that it could take up to a year to notice improvements, but sometimes it could happen in only a matter of weeks. I was in a hurry and wanted the 'matter of weeks' results, I wanted to see an improvement right away. I kept sending reminder messages to weigh himself first thing in the morning and to let me know if he was putting on weight; there had been some weight loss along with the jaundice. He obliged, but I could sense that he was becoming a little frustrated. I wasn't sure if that was due to the lack of improvement in his condition or my persistent messages that reminded him that there wasn't. So, I asked.

'Am I bothering you with my messages? My reminder messages? And the articles?'

'No, but I don't want to be constantly thinking about my situation. I don't want it to become a daily battle.'

'And neither do I, but the diet is a pretty strict one, and if you're going to give it a shot you have to follow it closely.'

'I think of it as a process, and one that involves more than just diet. And I think I can get through it more easily if we're both on the same page. I'm happy to try the change of diet, but I don't want it be a daily challenge of do this, don't do that, eat this, don't eat that, and of checking my weight every day too. I don't want it to be a struggle, it's a journey.'

I could see his point, but I also saw the denial thing, again.

After only a few weeks he was continuing to lose weight, possibly from the restricted carbohydrate intake, but we couldn't know for certain. Even without the regular weigh-ins, it was becoming visible. Even he could see it. His pants were hanging loose, and he had to punch extra holes in his belt to keep them up. Again, he didn't talk about it, and it was as if he didn't notice it.

But everyone else did. When we walked along the street people noticed, and they stared, but for a different reason than earlier times. They were now staring at his noticeably yellow skin; it was almost a bright yellow. They were startled, and they couldn't look away. But again, he didn't seem to notice.

I knew that he was going to have to make the appointment with the gastroenterologist, and soon. We had to know what was going on. But he needed convincing and I couldn't do that, even though I tried. It turned out that it was the pharmacist at his local pharmacy who could. He was shopping for some vitamin supplements when he approached him and asked him if he was aware that he had jaundice. When he told me, it was almost with an expression of surprise that other people could see it ... but at the same time, there was acceptance. And that was a relief for me; finally, he saw what everyone else saw. He knew that he couldn't keep ignoring what was happening. He had to have further tests. He had to go to the hospital.

Chapter 13

$\mathcal{I}$ didn't go with him to the hospital appointment as it was going to involve a number of tests, including a liver biopsy, and they would most likely keep him in overnight; something he wasn't expecting or happy about. But he maintained, as usual, his sense of humour. His message to me that day:

> [J] They're talking about the dinner menu – I told them I didn't want to be here for that.

Then after a few minutes:

> [J] They're wanting to keep me overnight! I'm putting my case forward. I didn't sign up for the army! I'm concerned about my car being on the road overnight. Plus, I'm bored. Extremely bored.

I replied:

> **[I]** You've got your iPad, listen to a podcast. And you can call me! It's only one night.

I knew Jev was not going to be the ideal patient, and that's why he'd resisted the idea of medical intervention. He liked doing his own thing; something he'd been doing all along. He'd had quite a few blood tests by the end of the day, and after the final one he'd had enough:

> **[J]** Just had another blood test, I've lost count of how many. I'm surprised I don't need a transfusion! And my arm is starting to look like a junkie's!

Later that night he sent a photo of his dinner, and it looked good, something he wasn't expecting either. He wrote a note of appreciation and attached it to the tray:

> *Thanks for that! It was a really tasty and nourishing dinner!*

It was thoughtful of him, and I was sure the kitchen staff would have thought so too.

He seemed to be in a better mood in the morning, a more appreciative mood. He sent me a message first thing:

> **[J]** That meal last night, and meeting the lovely head nurse and chatting with her, and the sun coming up outside my window this morning bathing the room in morning light, have all been little moments of joy.

[I] Yes, it's a reminder that there are always things to be grateful for. The gratitude attitude.

[J] Yeah, you're right.

[I] You see, I can sometimes be right! Thanks for acknowledging!

I tried the humour thing too, it helped. As did little moments of joy. And it was what he needed to remember – what we both needed to remember.

After the test results came through later in morning, there was no ignoring the fact that his PSC was progressing and his liver was showing signs of inflammation and scarring, and there was narrowing of the bile ducts that caused the build-up of bile and his jaundice. There was nothing they could do to treat him; he needed to be referred to the liver transplant clinic at the Austin Hospital, the only hospital in Melbourne that performed transplants. It was over an hour away from Healesville but only a ten-minute drive from my place. An appointment was made for him in a week's time. Suddenly decisions were being made *for* him – that's what being a patient involved. And that's what he didn't like, but had to accept.

Now things were going in an unanticipated – and unwelcome - direction, and at a pace faster than he wanted. Appointment after appointment followed test after test. Jev was now absorbed into the healthcare system, and being part of that meant an unbearable loss of autonomy. He continued his alternative practices, but he was beginning to realise he was delaying the inevitable. A liver transplant was his only option and that was something I knew he didn't want. In the end, he called Warren to let him know what was happening and to discuss a plan of attack, but there was no plan.

Even armed with the test results, Warren's only suggestion to this emaciated man so clearly in the throes of liver failure was to increase his Qigong to three times a day and to see him for acupuncture once a week! I was so stunned I could hardly speak.

I was looking at successful liver transplant stories on the hospital website and found Jas, someone who had the same condition as Jev. He had been diagnosed with PSC as a young adult and, like Jev, it was only many years later that it started to become a serious health issue; it had progressed to the point where a liver transplant was the necessary next step. As he put it, he became 'one of the lucky ones'; after about fourteen months of waiting he got a new liver, and a new life. He became the hospital's seven hundred and eighty-fifth liver transplant recipient. And his recovery story after the transplant was inspiring, no other word for it.

Five months after the operation he went on a 4km run and sixteen months after he completed a 100km bike ride from Sorrento to Melbourne. Then he joined a running team and kept extending his running distances – his next run would be the Melbourne Marathon. That I *had* to share with Jev, and he was inspired. He was slowly coming to accept the prospect of having to have the transplant, and reading stories like Jas's would help. He needed to hear the success stories.

The appointment at the Austin was at 9:00 in the morning. He stayed at my place the night before to avoid driving in heavy morning traffic, which would have made an hour trip closer to two hours. We got up early, had breakfast, and got ready to go. He always carried a snack with him in case he got hungry, but also to keep up his calorie intake.

It didn't take him long to get dressed; track pants and a casual top with a zip up hoodie. I remembered the way he used to stand in front of the mirror to check his appearance before going out: crisp tight-fitting black shirt sitting over his slim fit rust-coloured pants, with black leather lace up shoes. The way he stood, looking in the mirror with one hand on his hip and one knee slightly bent, his 'checking himself out' pose. Perhaps there was a touch of vanity, but he looked good. He was a tall, slim, well-dressed, good-looking man. And he saw that in the mirror. After his recent weight loss and jaundice, he didn't spend so much time choosing an outfit or looking in the mirror. What he saw reflected back at him was a reminder of how much he'd changed, and how little he could do to change things back.

We walked to the station at the end of my street and caught the train to Heidelberg Station. I'd checked the night before and found that it was just a five-minute trip, and the hospital was just across the road. No traffic, no car parking hassles, and no stress. It was only later that I thought more about that, about the synchronicity of events that brought Jev here, with me. I'd read that sometimes people had to relocate to be closer to the hospital. Distance was a factor in getting onto the transplant list.

Visiting a hospital can be a confronting experience, but during Covid it was even more so. We had to line up in a queue and sign in: name and reason for visit. We were given new masks to wear and an ID sticker to attach to our clothing, and then told to take the lift to the fifth floor and follow the blue line to the liver clinic. Sitting in the waiting room with other people waiting to be seen, I couldn't help but do what the people on the street did when they saw Jev; I noticed who was looking yellow and who was looking very underweight. I tried not to stare but I couldn't help but compare Jev and these other patients. Who would be activated on the list, and who wouldn't? Who would be chosen for a new liver? Who was in greater need? Who might be too sick to get on the list?

Meeting the doctor was the first step in the assessment process. We didn't have to wait long; she appeared around a corner and called Jev's name. We sat in a small room, the chairs set well apart. She was young and friendly and once she heard that Jev was an English teacher she seemed to take a greater interest in him, English was one of her favourite subjects at school. She then explained the assessment process in more detail. There would be a number of tests assessing his physical health, including heart and lung function; a visit with a dietician to look at diet and maintaining a healthy weight; and a visit with a psychiatrist to assess mental wellbeing and social supports, which included family and friends. She checked his weight and made a point of telling him that if he lost too much weight it would exclude him from being considered for a transplant, but the dietician would talk more about making changes to his diet and including high calorie foods to help keep his weight up. Going through a transplant required maintaining a certain level of physical health in order to be able to deal with the sometimes long pre-transplant waiting period and the post-transplant recovery.

It also required a support team; he couldn't do it alone. She asked him if he had a group of people that he could call on should he need help. She wanted more than a yes – she wanted names, and to know if they were family members or friends. He said he'd have a think and get back to her. She then asked him who his main carer would be. Without looking at me, he pointed his thumb my way. No words were spoken.

She organised the tests for the following week. If he was considered to be a suitable candidate – and she was optimistic that he would be – he would be activated on the transplant waiting list. She explained that it wasn't a chronological list where you work your way down from the top to the bottom. There were other factors to be considered and the most important was finding a suitable match, which included blood type, body size, and age. And then the urgency of the need for a transplant, how sick a patient was – but being too sick would be a problem. Deteriorating health could mean being excluded from the transplant list.

She also explained the risks and complications during and after the operation. There was a 1 in 100 risk of dying during the operation, and there was also the risk of the body rejecting the new liver after the operation. That wasn't so encouraging to hear, but the success rate stats were. The one-year survival rate was approximately ninety-three per cent, and eighty-six percent for five years. And there were cases of transplant recipients living beyond thirty years. I could see

Jev's expression change when he heard that. Yes, the process would be an ordeal, but once it was over he could make plans for the future. He could do what he'd been thinking of doing, retiring from full-time teaching and pursuing his music and art. It really would be a new life.

The average waiting period was eight to twelve months, but with Covid and lockdowns it would most likely extend beyond that. The unfortunate truth was that there were fewer donors; in other words, demand outstripped supply. She didn't say, but it suddenly hit me that someone had to die in order for a liver to become available. Fewer people out and about and on the roads meant fewer deaths on the road. That was a hard thing to fathom; the need for someone to die, even in a car accident, so that someone else could live. But that's the only way the transplant could happen. It truly was a gift, a gift of hope.

On the way home, I asked Jev whom he would ask to be part of his support team, as he was going to have to come up with a list. There was his son, a friend he had known in New Zealand, now also living in Melbourne, and possibly a colleague at work. His other close friends lived interstate. That was only three people. He was going to have to reach out to others, not something he did easily. I encouraged him to start thinking about it and start asking.

Chapter 14

I kept revisiting the conversation with the doctor – in particular, what she said about the need for a support team. Without one he wouldn't be accepted on to the transplant list. That, and the fact that he nominated me as his main carer without asking me. I didn't like that he didn't ask me; and I was a little surprised that he would simply assume such a thing. That he wouldn't ask exactly what the role involved. That he didn't consider all the practicalities. That he didn't consider my needs. That he didn't turn to me when the doctor asked the question and say, 'I need to talk to Ida about that.' We weren't husband and wife and we weren't living together. We had been dating for just under two years. I wasn't sure what being a main carer involved, and we both needed to know. Why didn't he ask? Why didn't I?

I decided it was best to talk to him about it, to tell him how I was feeling. It was after dinner one night at my place. We'd just had a takeaway Vietnamese meal. After hearing what the doctor said about maintaining a healthy weight, he decided that restricting carbohydrates on the Paleo diet was causing him to lose too much weight, and he started reintroducing foods that he enjoyed, and that were high in calories.

'I've been thinking about our meeting with the doctor, and about being your main carer. I'm not sure I'm comfortable with that term. I'm not really sure I know what it means or what it involves. And I think I need to know, we both do.'

His reaction took me by surprise. Suddenly, he looked afraid. He immediately covered his face with his hands and took a deep breath. He didn't say anything for a while. He seemed stunned. And I felt awful; I didn't intend to upset him, I just wanted to talk about it, to be open about how I felt. I just wanted some clarity.

'I'm going to have to let them know.' He didn't look at me, he kept rubbing his face with his hands, as if he was trying to get rid of whatever it was that he was feeling; a flush of colour and fear. Something I'd never seen in him before.

I reached across the table and took his hand. 'Hey, I think you've misunderstood. I just mean that I'd feel more comfortable if I understood better what's involved, and if there were other people you could call on, whom I could call on too. We don't live together, and I live an hour away. I'm not sure how I can be a main carer if we don't live together. That's not something we've talked about, and we need to. And I need to know exactly what's expected of me. Surely you can see that. Then there's my work – how can I continue working and caring for you? I think a team is what we need, it's what the doctor said – a support team. It can't be just the two of us.'

Again, a deep breath. 'Yeah, you're right, you're right. I have to start working on that.'

It was one of those *I have no other choice* realisations. But there were possibilities and I tried to make him understand that. 'I thought you might ask your ex-wife to be part of the team, but I'm not sure how you feel about that. I have read that exes often step up in situations like this. They want to help.'

'Nah, I don't think so. I haven't spoken to her since the divorce. Not sure I want to be asking her any favours right now.'

He had his estranged sister too; I was going to suggest he contact her, but I could see that was also unlikely to happen. I had considered calling her myself, but Jev would have to know. And he wouldn't like it. I'm not sure what caused their falling-out. He told me that she didn't like him, that she told him that she didn't. I couldn't imagine how that conversation went, but they stopped talking and he hadn't seen her in years. She lived locally, as did his ex. That was a huge plus, to be part of his support team and to live close by. His sister probably knew he was unwell. If she knew, she wasn't reaching out. Sometimes rifts can continue and fester, forever. But I held out a small hope that she might agree to be part of the team. He needed her.

He was quiet the rest of the evening. I felt as though I'd let him down. But I wasn't deserting him, I wasn't. He was alone, that was his problem. He didn't have a network of family and friends around him. To be alone and unwell, *seriously* unwell

... not a good combination. I had a friend who always said, 'We need to be able to ask for help, and most people are willing to lend a hand if they're asked.'

The not reaching out was the problem, and that was what Jev found so difficult, even with me. I spent the rest of the evening feeling alone. All I wanted was for him to wrap his arms around me, like he used to do, and tell me that it would all work out, that we would work things out together – we were, after all, a team – and that he loved me and we would get through this together. But instead, we didn't talk for the rest of the evening. We had an early night and he left to go home first thing the next day.

And then came the week of appointments at the hospital to assess his suitability for a transplant. He took time off work and spent the week at my place. He caught the train in the morning and I sometimes picked him up, depending on whether I was working or not. Even though he was beginning to feel more fatigue as his condition progressed, catching the train didn't exhaust him; it was the time spent at the hospital that did. It was the long periods of waiting between tests, and nothing ever happened on time. It was a long week that included medical tests to assess his physical health, interviews with a psychiatrist, a social worker, and a dietician. By the end of the week he was exhausted but also relieved; he had been activated on the liver transplant waiting list. It was a strange thing; we wanted to celebrate, to acknowledge that he was now on the way to a new life, but it didn't quite feel right. There was still a long way to go.

He was told that he could get a call from the hospital at any time and that he should be prepared. Once he got the call he would have to leave right away, and he couldn't be more than two hours away from the hospital. That meant he had to have a suitcase packed and ready with the things he would need for a longer stay; he needed to be ready to go. And he was told to have his phone switched on and with him at all times. That was the challenging part for Jev – he didn't carry his phone with him all the time, and he wasn't one to constantly check his messages. His phone would sit on the kitchen table and he would move from room to room doing whatever he needed to. I would sometimes call and he didn't answer, then call his landline and still no answer. And that could no longer happen. He would also forget to take it with him when he went to bed. That also had to change.

So, I started sending reminder messages again, to keep his phone turned on and with him at all times. He thought it was too soon to be getting a call from the transplant team; I thought that wasn't the point, he had to start preparing, changing some habits, and start expecting a call. He was, as always, a little too relaxed about it all. But I knew that life was on hold until he got that call.

I was beginning to feel a little in need of support myself. And I could have reached out to the social worker at the liver clinic, but instead I went to see someone who knew me better. I went to see Janet, a counsellor I had visited during my separation. After friends, she was the person I turned to. We had quite a few sessions together and we got to know each other well. We talked about the reasons I was leaving my marriage, and my need to reclaim my life. She told me about her mother having done the same thing. I continued to see her even after I'd moved out and started dating. Sometimes it felt as if I was visiting a friend, a very understanding friend. Our sessions came to an end just as my new life was beginning.

When I went back to see her, it was to tell her about Jev's illness. She didn't look at me and express her sympathy, or surprise. She simply said, 'You're under no obligation to stay. You're not married and yours isn't a long-term relationship. There are other options.'

I was a little startled by her matter-of-fact response, but I knew she was thinking about me. She knew about my post-divorce journey into a new life; she didn't want me to take a step backwards. And she knew I'd been the full-time carer for my elderly parents. And that's where I was heading again, full-time carer.

I left thinking about what she'd said, about considering my options carefully. And what were those options? One was to get out now. I couldn't lose what I'd just recently gained, my freedom. The other was stay and look after him. We'd been together almost two years. We'd had some good times together, fun times. We loved each other. Jev had been good for me. And now I needed to be good to him.

Both options were valid. Both were possible. Both were reasonable. But was there really a choice?

Chapter 15

It didn't surprise me to hear that Jev had months of accumulated sick leave; he seldom took days off, not even sick days. But things had changed. He didn't have the energy to continue teaching and he had to take time off – extended time off. He wasn't sleeping at night, which was a common problem with people suffering from advanced liver cirrhosis. He might get an hour or two of sleep and then lie awake for the rest of the night. He'd listen to podcasts, and sometimes get up and play his guitar or draw. He'd crash the next day and spend most of it in bed, not sleeping, just resting. It left him feeling drained and weary. It always surprised me that he could keep functioning, and he did. He would still drive to Fairfield, still attend his medical appointments, but he'd have to have regular rest periods during the day.

Life had changed. It became a blur of medical appointments and tests and hospital stays. It wasn't a matter of sitting back and waiting for the call; they had to monitor the progression of his liver damage. We knew that if he got too sick, he couldn't have the transplant. The 'too sick' comment stuck in my mind, so my life became obsessive searching for information about liver cirrhosis in people with PSC, and constant monitoring of his symptoms. I didn't send Jev the entire articles, I knew he wouldn't read them, so I just sent relevant sections. His reply was, 'Science-y', and then he would send me a series of drawings he'd just completed and was going to get framed. I stopped searching for articles. But I didn't stop worrying and checking on him and sending reminders. As his main carer, that was the least of my duties. But Jev wasn't always so understanding, and sometimes he expressed his irritation. It was a phone conversation where I again asked him where he had his phone, as I'd tried to call him earlier.

'Did you say that you don't need me to 'shepherd' you around?' I asked.

'Sheepdog.'

'What does that mean?'

'I appreciate you being by my side but sometimes I feel like I'm being watched and supervised, even from a distance. And sometimes I feel like you don't listen to me, that you aren't making space for me to talk. In your head you're already formulating the next thing.'

'The next thing to help you.'

'Yeah, I know you're trying to help but I get enough telling from the hospital, having to follow their instructions. I don't need that all the time. Sometimes I just need to take a break.'

I wasn't sure what he wanted me to do instead. As his main carer, what did he think I should be doing? He didn't say and I didn't ask. And I didn't like that he didn't acknowledge how he needed the reminders, the suggestions, the help. He didn't seem to understand that he really couldn't do it alone.

The way we spent our time together changed too. We no longer went on little adventures, we rarely went out at all; no long walks in the forest or the parklands, or walks along the beach, no train rides, no op shop visits, no bookshops, no games of billiards at a local café, and no grocery shopping excursions. We did go for short walks, as Jev had to try and maintain some fitness and muscle mass, but it wasn't the same. He occupied his time with music, listening to podcasts, and working on his art and photography; even when we were together. I was beginning to feel invisible, something I had only experienced during my marriage.

And what did I do while he was doing those solo things? While he was scouring the internet looking for a podcast to listen to, I did my own search for high calorie recipes that wouldn't upset his sensitive digestion. While he was doing his drawings, I busied myself with household chores. While he played the guitar, I sat trying to read a book. While he had a nap, I went for a walk. And if I lay down to rest with him, we didn't touch; there was a space between us on the bed. Sometimes I'd reach across and take his hand but he didn't move closer. He always stayed completely still. There was no longer any physical intimacy.

I knew that another symptom of liver disease was impotency. That was something else I learned through my reading. Jev realised what was happening but he didn't talk to me about it, he simply withdrew. When he stayed over at my place, he slept in the spare room. The constant wakefulness was his reason, he didn't want to disturb my sleep. But it saddened me that we couldn't maintain some level of closeness without the sex. Just lying together, holding each other, would have been enough. When I did try to give him a hug, it was only a very brief one. I think it made him feel uncomfortable, a reminder of how he had changed. And he had. The strong arms that once held me in a tight embrace were now thin and wasted. When I wrapped my arms around him, even for those few brief moments, I felt his ribs protruding and the frailness of his body. He was disappearing, slowly.

And our relationship changed too; there were fewer expressions of affection, both physical and emotional. He had stopped doing my hair; no more regular trims and blow waves. It felt like another loss. He would always be the one checking my hair and assessing it, always the one to suggest a 'visit' to the hairdresser. He used to enjoy it as much as I did. A session under the cape always preceded a session in the bedroom; it was like foreplay for him. Maybe that too was a reminder of the change in him. A change that he found hard to deal with, and to talk about.

During one of my Google searches, I read that just talking with a partner about ways to keep intimacy alive was a way of being intimate. I thought that was better than nothing, and it was worth trying. We were sitting in my courtyard in the sunshine. I found that being outside, or being on a walk, made talking easier; conversation seemed to flow more. I started gently by acknowledging that it was a difficult time for him, for both of us. That we were both having to adjust to the changed circumstances, but that didn't have to include changes in our relationship.

He looked blankly at me and said, 'You don't get it.'

'I'm trying to, and that's why I think we need to keep talking, keep communicating. Sometimes it feels like there's a wall between us and I sometimes feel invisible, and that makes me feel a little depressed.'

Again, the blank stare. 'You expect me to make you feel better, but that's not my responsibility.'

Even though that was true, it wasn't the most loving thing to say. 'That's not what I'm saying. So much has changed in such a short time. Everything is different.'

'What are you trying to say?' He looked at me with an expression of alarm. I got the impression that he thought I was trying to tell him that I wanted out of the relationship. Maybe it was a reminder of past experiences, being rejected by his parents and his wife.

I wasn't happy. I was depressed, I was feeling invisible, and I'd had enough. But I didn't want to upset him, and that's what I told him, and the conversation stopped there. He continued working on his iPad, and I went inside to make a cup of tea, trying not to think about what just happened; the failed attempt at moving closer together.

Maybe he was right. Maybe I couldn't understand what it was like to live every day facing the challenges he did. Maybe I needed to stop and think about that. And maybe he needed to stop and think about what I might be going through, to try and understand the changes in my life. It was his detachment that disturbed me the most. I couldn't understand how he didn't try to include me in whatever it was that he was feeling, to talk about it with me, to share his feelings. Then I remembered what my doctor had said when I last visited her and she asked about Jev: 'A sick person's world shrinks.' I was beginning to understand what she meant.

It was a Thursday, and he'd spent the day at the hospital having blood transfusions. His recent blood test had shown a very low blood count. He had been experiencing excessive fatigue and some confusion the day before; I called the liver clinic to organise for a pathology slip to be emailed to him, and without delay he went off to have an urgent blood test. When the results came in later that day, he got a call from the transplant coordinator telling him that he needed to get to the hospital as soon as possible. It was almost like a trial transplant call run; no warning, just grab your things and get in the car.

By the time he got to my place it was 8:00 on the Wednesday night, and I drove him straight to the emergency department. He knew it was going to be an overnight stay, and that was something he dreaded. They discharged him on Thursday, but he was feeling very tired after the endless blood tests, transfusions, and no sleep. We both knew he couldn't drive back to Healesville. After having a nap and dinner he was still looking unwell, and I suggested taking him back to the hospital to get his blood levels checked again, but he simply refused and went to bed saying he just needed to sleep. I was working the next day and went to bed early, as well.

I heard him get up in the middle of the night to use the toilet; that wasn't unusual, but then I heard him moaning. I got up and found him holding onto the wall in the hallway, unable to move. He was bent over and struggling to speak, his speech was slurred. 'I need the toilet.'

I immediately knew what was happening – more blood loss from internal bleeding; bleeding varices caused low blood pressure, and light-headedness. I helped him to the toilet and he had a bowel motion. The stools were black and tarry, another sign of internal bleeding. I helped him wipe his bottom and then helped him back to bed. He was moaning, and it was a struggle to walk. He sat on the edge of the bed but he couldn't stay upright – he fell back in a slump. I knew it was a medical emergency and that if the bleeding continued he could go into shock and lose consciousness. I told him I was going to call an ambulance and still he resisted; he didn't want to spend hours back in emergency. I grabbed my phone and made the call.

The ambulance arrived within minutes, and while they were getting Jev into a wheelchair I quickly packed a few things for him: his phone and charger, his iPad, his toiletries, and some clothes. It was 4:00 on Friday morning and he was in the ambulance on his way to hospital.

I stayed up, and after an hour I checked in with the emergency department. He was being admitted and he would be having more blood transfusions. I decided to go to work as there was nothing else I could do. And as a casual relief teacher, calling in sick wouldn't be a good thing. I was the one replacing sick teachers. While I was at school, I kept checking my phone for a message from Jev. It finally came later in the morning:

> [J] Blood count 55 – even lower than last time. It explains the symptoms.
>
> [I] Of course, it does. But what are they saying needs to be done?
>
> [J] More transfusions and then they'll have to figure out how to stop the bleeding.
>
> [I] Okay, hope you had something to eat.
>
> [J] Can't, I'm about to head into transfusion world and then the gastro camera. Waiting to get the go ahead to eat and drink. Very weak. Signing off now to rest. Text later. XX

I called the hospital at lunch time, and then messaged Jev:

> [I] I just spoke to the nurse, Susan, she's lovely. You need to eat! I told her you hadn't eaten much for a couple of days. They're trying to get the okay from the doctor, and the dietician will be seeing you too. Let me know when you've had something to eat. Xx
>
> [J] Clear fluids again until midnight, then fasting. Having gastroscopy and colonoscopy tomorrow.

I knew it was going to be a long stay and a difficult one, and he would be having his birthday in hospital. Not what I'd planned. Thankfully, there wasn't a lockdown and I would be able to visit him. During the last lockdown, hospital visits were not allowed and there were instances of people dying without a family member present. As one report described it, it was brutal.

I wrote him a card and set off for the hospital on the Sunday morning. My card was nowhere near as arty as the one he'd made for my birthday just a few months after we first met. I got a glimpse then of his creative streak, and his originality. Apart from my son when he was young, no one had ever gone to that much trouble. He'd included some photos of me that he'd taken; some I was unaware of. There was one on the front of the card where I had my head tilted to the side, my finger touching my mouth in a thinking pose. He added a large colourful question mark at the top of the photo, and at the bottom the words, 'Some people reach fifty-eight and they're in a quandary.' Inside, there was a second photo with my finger now in the air and looking as though I'd come to a realisation. He added a drawing of a light bulb at the top and at the bottom the words, 'But if you're lucky, a light bulb goes on ...' And the third photo I was posing with my hands in my jeans pockets and wearing one of his hats. 'And they realise that they can be chic and cool at any age ...' The photo at the back was of the two of us looking blissfully happy. 'Happy Birthday, Beautiful!' was written in large colourful letters. I was amazed, and pleased, at the effort he'd gone to. No Hallmark card, a handmade, beautiful card instead.

As I entered the ward, I asked for directions to Jev's room. The woman I asked looked at me and said, 'You're Ida.' I was confused. Did I know her? I was wearing a mask; how did she recognise me? And then I recalled her voice – I knew that voice. It was Laura, the social worker. We had spoken many times over the phone, and she was the most delightful person, so understanding and helpful and kind. She had become almost a friend; the whole liver transplant unit had become like an extended family. They were always available to talk, always supportive and encouraging. We stood and spoke for a while, and she told me that she'd be checking in with Jev later on, and that she'd wish him a happy birthday too.

There were other patients chatting to their visitors in Jev's room. The curtains were closed around the bed in the corner of the room; I drew them aside and saw Jev lying fully clothed, wearing an eye mask to block the bright lights. He was still, his hands crossed over his chest. I sat beside the bed and watched him, his chest rising and falling with each breath. I didn't want to disturb him, but I gently whispered his name to check if he was sleeping. He was.

I sat for a while longer, my hand gently resting on his leg. He looked tired and drawn. The hospital stays always took it out of him, and understandably so. This time it had been one of the toughest. As he put it in his message the night before:

> [J] This week has been one of the worst in my life and last night really stretched me to the limits. Tell you about it tomorrow.

But I had to remind him of something:

> [I] You're strong, you'll get through this. And then, as you said, let's not waste a minute.

Before leaving I propped the card against a glass on the bedside table where he would see it when he woke up. And when he opened it, he would read:

> 'Dear Jev, the journey we've been on these past few months has been a difficult one, but your resilience and equanimity have been an inspiration. May the years ahead be filled with good health, happiness and love.
>
> Happy birthday! Much love from me to you. Ida xxx'

Soon after I got home his response arrived:

> [J] Love the card. The journey will end in a bright future, eventually. And love you. xxx

Chapter 16

First thing the next day, I called and spoke to the transplant coordinator to get a better idea of what was happening with Jev. She told me that he was experiencing more bleeds than usual and that it was of concern, but the transfusions would bring his blood count up and then hopefully fewer bleeds. I told her about the rush to get him to hospital in the early hours of the morning and that he didn't want to go, but that I called an ambulance because I knew what was happening.

'That's because you're a good carer,' she said. 'You saved his life.'

And that's when I realised exactly what being a carer, a main carer, involved. Life and death decisions.

Laura called me soon after to ask about Jev's support team; he hadn't let her know who was in it. I wasn't surprised but she was worried. Time was passing and he was moving up the list, but not having the right support would affect his chances of getting a call should a matching donor become available. I reassured her that he had spoken to a few people, and that there were four people on his list. She was relieved to hear that, and she would let the transplant coordinator know.

He *had* asked a few people, and they were all happy to help out both pre- or post-transplant. His colleague at work said, 'It would be a privilege.' And then there was his son, and a friend he had known in New Zealand; he didn't live nearby but he was happy to be included as part of the team, and would help in any way he could. And then there was me.

He'd told me in one of his messages that he'd been doing a bit of thinking while he was in hospital; he didn't have a lot else he could do.

> **[J]** Once I get through this, I'll be changing my lifestyle, and I'll be a much freer agent. And I've been thinking about us. It's an outdated and rather conventional and narrowminded view that to be a couple you have to live together all the time. It's more important that the couple is at a similar life stage, has similar educational and life experience backgrounds.

> **[I]** What do you mean when you say you're going to be a 'freer agent'? How will that change things?

> **[J]** Reduced work hours and no responsibilities. Less structured work means more freedom, and work becomes purely a means to make dosh. I'll have the flexibility and freedom to do other things without being encumbered by bells and timetables. Whether that be playing gigs on the local scene, doing my

art, or hanging out with you and going for rides on our scooter. I guess the symbol that represents our journey after the transplant op, and my new phase of life with you, is the Peugeot scooter. A sense of freedom and adventure.

I wasn't sure if riding a scooter was a 'little' adventure, but I was willing to give it a go.

[I] I like your thinking, and I'm prepared to expand my little adventures to include riding a scooter together!

[J] Yes, together. XXX

I was happy that he'd been thinking about us, about a future together. As his illness progressed, a distance crept in. We lost the connection we once had, and he was reluctant to talk about it.
And I wanted to.

He'd been back at home for a couple of weeks and feeling better after the last lot of blood transfusions. They had managed to stop the bleeding by wrapping the varices with an elastic band, but they were concerned about the frequency of the bleeds. Because the risk of re-bleeding in Jev was so high, they recommended he have another endoscopy soon, and they sent him regular pathology slips for blood tests. Any sign of a low blood count and he would have to go back to hospital, without delay.

It had been a little while since I'd been to Healesville; with his hospital visits he'd been spending more time at my place, so I took off one Sunday morning to spend the day with him. I didn't stay over as he didn't have a spare room set up, and sleeping together had become too difficult, for both of us, because of his insomnia.

I had missed the drive. I missed driving past the wineries and vineyards and being reminded of my time in Tuscany. I missed the long stretches of country roads and the morning mist rising in the hills. I missed the farmhouses nestled among trees. I missed leaving the city behind. It was during a lockdown period, and I had to stop at a police checkpoint as there were restrictions in place as to what we could and couldn't do.

One of the restrictions was that we had to stay within five kilometres of our residence. Visiting an 'intimate partner' was one of the exemptions from that rule. I stopped, rolled down my window, and waited for the question I'd heard many times before.

'What's your reason for being here today?'

'I'm visiting my partner in Healesville.'

'And what's the nature of the relationship?'

That question always made me hesitate, and smile. 'I'm visiting my boyfriend. I feel a bit a bit odd saying that at my age, but that's what he is.'

The police officer smiled and, after checking my driver's licence, he wished me a good day, and off I went. To visit my boyfriend.

He was still not sleeping well and had limited energy. We still couldn't go for long walks but he could manage little walks around the township. We visited the weekend community market at Coronation Park and picked up some locally-grown organic produce. And afterwards we went for a walk by the creek, stopping along the way to sit on a bench in the sun. It was gentle and relaxing, but still he needed to have a rest as soon as we got back home. And then again after lunch. We lay on the bed together and, as I turned on my side, he moved towards me and wrapped his arms around me. He held me tight, and we lay there without speaking. I felt again the connection we once had; our bodies together, merged as one. As we gently stroked each other, his hands became mine, and mine his. If I looked at his hands, I saw mine. They had become indistinguishable. I felt happy again, calm and happy. Maybe it was the rush of endorphins, maybe it was me reliving in my mind how this scenario would have once panned out. But it was enough that he was holding me.

When I left later in the afternoon, he walked me to my car. Just before getting in, I turned to him and said, 'You know it's going to happen. The waiting won't go on for too much longer. When I spoke to Laura, she said they review each case regularly and that it was looking promising for you. I asked her how long and she said maybe only four or so months. That's soon. It's going to happen soon, and that's what we've been waiting for. Remember that.'

I saw a hint of a small smile and his expression softened. The weariness, the burdensome uncertainty, lifted for a few brief moments as he registered what I was saying. The transplant would happen soon. He needed to hear that. He would be released from the lingering wait. He would have the energy to do things again. He would be himself again. We would be us again.

When I got home, I sent him a message to let him know I had arrived safely, as I used to do:

> [I] Back now. It was good to see you, to be back in Healesville, and to be lying in your arms again. xxx
>
> [J] Yeah, I totally agree. A brilliant day. Thanks for coming. Xx

It had been a good day, a better day than usual. The feeling of closeness had returned. After a sense of disconnect over the past few months, it was good to be with the Jev of old again. Being physically close felt good, felt right. Why he had avoided it for so long I couldn't quite understand – even without sex there can be physical closeness, and that's what, in his personal definition of 'sexual being', Jev struggled with. That's what he identified with, his sexuality; he was a man who enjoyed having sex, enjoyed having lots of sex. And enjoyed pleasing women. With the loss of libido, he had to face a Jev he didn't recognise, or perhaps even like. He was no longer Mr T, the much-respected teacher, and no longer the man who could gratify women sexually; two labels he was strongly attached to. Who was he without them? Instead of exploring other options, he seemed to be lost, and he stayed lost.

I knew what it was like to feel invisible, but it wasn't the same as the *me* in a loveless marriage; I still loved Jev and wanted to be with him. Sometimes it seemed that wasn't enough for him, it wasn't a life he could, or even *wanted* to try and accept – even with me in it. Not even love could replace his loss. He once told me that he didn't have the energy for it, but to me, to let love in doesn't take effort. It doesn't deplete and exhaust. No, it nourishes, and it energises. I always thought it took more energy to close your heart.

When illness grows, it can overtake your life. It can become a life versus death existence and just living, a diminished living, in order not to die. The living isn't pleasure-based, it's about what to eat and what not to eat, whom to consult and new therapies and supplements to trial, tests and procedures and medications; all in order to stay alive. Yes, a sick person's world can shrink, if they allow it to.

Chapter 17

The illness, once again, took centre stage.

After only a few weeks Jev was back at the hospital after a blood test revealed a very low blood count. And they had been a good few weeks where he spent more time walking in nature and playing music and sitting on the deck in the sunshine, feeling a little more optimistic about his future. But being back in emergency waiting to be assessed made him realise that it wasn't quite over yet. The journey continued.

It was going to be an overnight stay, and most likely longer depending on what the tests revealed. In all the uncertainty that made up his days, there was one thing that was certain – the internal bleeding hadn't stopped. That was worrying the doctors, and if it continued it could cause complications. And it was wearing him out. He needed to maintain a certain level of fitness and good health to be able to deal with the actual transplant surgery.

He was most likely going to have to have another endoscopy, which involved having a general anaesthetic. The good thing was that they could treat the bleeding at the same time, no need for another procedure. But still, the aftereffects of the anaesthetic stayed with him for days and added to his fatigue. I sent a message asking for an update:

> [J] Nothing has happened yet. Spoke to the dietician about muscle wastage, she suggested using weights. Might get some light ones for walking when I get out of jail.

And with no visitors allowed that's how it felt: like being locked up in jail. He kept sending me regular updates to let me know how things were going, and sometimes a call:

> [J] Blood count still low, having more transfusions. Had the camera pill last night, should get results soon.
>
> [J] They gave me something that made me poo in the bed. Now wearing undies from my washing bag!
>
> [J] Ankles and stomach swollen, hard to walk. They're going to try and drop the fluid through meds, more meds! Still waiting on the camera pill data. So, no knowledge yet about the source of the bleeding.
>
> [J] Just overheard the guy in the next bed – a black dude with a serious accent. He's a bass player so I introduced myself. We have a lot in common as far as music goes. He had a transplant in 2005 and said it was a million-dollar fresh start. Let's try and remember that and keep a positive approach. He's looking good too. Just in for some routine tests.
>
> [J] Colonoscopy moved to top priority in the morning. Here we go again.

[J] Here's a kicker, they put an announcement out from maintenance last night that the system was malfunctioning and so the air conditioning was on all night. It still is, so the place is fucking freezing. I'm wearing my jacket in bed. Gotta get out of here! Xx

[J] I started the process of having phone conversations with people last night. I've asked them to send me a text telling me when a good time to chat is. I sent the messages to Hannah, Marianne and Nick. A good suggestion, thanks. Xx

[J] Just about to have an afternoon nap. Talk later. Xx

[J] Didn't get much sleep. There's an immature, crude and disgusting Greek dude who's visiting his mother. Wearing a track suit, complaining to the nurses, always on phone, dumb as dog shit. How did these people produce Aristotle and Pythagorean geometry??

[J] Feeling very tired. Signing off now. Sleep well and talk tomorrow. Xx

The strange thing was that when he was in hospital, I stopped worrying about him. I knew he was safe. I knew he would have nurses checking on him regularly. He wouldn't have a fall trying to negotiate his steep drive, which had happened. I wasn't going to have to monitor his comings and goings. I didn't have to keep checking that his phone was on and with him. I knew he was where he needed to be. I almost felt a sense of relief. He was being looked after, and I could breathe easy for a while.

After the procedure he was given more blood transfusions and, once his blood count improved, he was able to leave. Before leaving, they strongly recommended that he have a Covid vaccination; they were recommending that everyone on the waiting list have one. After the transplant he would be given anti-rejection drugs, immunosuppressants, to stop his body rejecting the new liver. These drugs weakened the immune system, which made it easier to pick up infections, and more difficult for the body to deal with them. That's why vaccinations were necessary. He'd already been given vaccinations for chicken pox, TB, and hepatitis. The transplant coordinator called me and asked that I let her know once he'd had the Covid one. I got the impression that without it, his chances of getting a new liver might be affected. There were fewer donors and they were doing all they could to make sure the transplants were a success; that they were going to recipients that ticked all the boxes. A new liver was a gift and it couldn't be wasted. I called his local doctor to see if he was offering vaccinations, and he was. Jev would have to call and make an appointment when he got home, so there wouldn't be any delay.

After I got Jev's text message that he was being discharged, or 'released from jail' as he put it, I stopped what I was doing, got in the car, and went to pick him up. As soon as I saw him standing outside the emergency entrance, I knew that he was feeling the usual post-hospital visit weariness. He was leaning against the outside wall with shoulders slumped and head bent forward, his red backpack at his feet. When he got in the front seat his head fell back and his eyes closed. There was little conversation, but I asked him about the vaccination and he agreed that it was a good idea to have one.

When we got back to my place, he went straight to bed with a hot water bottle and stayed there for a couple of hours. I was a little worried as it was getting late and he needed to have something to eat. I opened the door to check if he was still sleeping. He was lying on his back, perfectly still, with the covers up to his chin. He felt the cold more than usual and needed an extra doona to keep warm.

I sat on the edge of the bed and softly called his name. He didn't respond. I put my hand gently on his shoulder and tried again. He took a deep breath. I didn't want to wake him – after all the prodding and poking at the hospital, he was enjoying what he needed, some undisturbed rest. But he had to eat.

'It's getting late. You probably should get up and have something to eat. I've made chicken soup.'

He nodded and opened his eyes. He looked at me with a lifeless, blank expression. I felt overcome by a sense of despair. I wanted to see him smile, to see some hope in his eyes, but all I saw was weariness.

Soon after dinner, he was back in bed. I was working the next day and he would be heading back to Healesville in the morning. I suggested that he stay but he was expecting a package, a book he'd ordered, and he wanted to be home. I knew there wasn't much he could do at my place, no studio set up with his musical equipment, and no deck with views of the hills. And he had to have the jab. He knew that there might be some soreness and fatigue for a few days afterwards and probably felt more comfortable crashing at his place. And I was working the rest of the week; he was conscious of giving me space. After a day of teaching, I was pretty wrecked.

We were both up early, and after breakfast he decided to 'get out of my way' as he put it, so I could get myself ready for work. His car was parked on the street and I walked him down the driveway. I'd packed a few groceries and leftover dinner for him to take. He wouldn't need to stop and do shopping; he could get home and not worry about having to cook for a few days. As Jev was getting into the car, my Italian neighbour, Domenico, walked by on his early morning walk. He was a lovely man in his early eighties and whenever we crossed paths we always stopped to have a chat in Italian.

I turned to wave and say hello, and he smiled, a warm smile, and I couldn't help but smile too. And then looking back at Jev I saw his unchanged expression, blank and sad. I didn't want him leaving like that. I leaned into the open window and smiled, telling him to smile too, that it would help lift his mood. He scowled instead. The smile disappeared from my face. I moved away quickly and went back inside. It wasn't what I was expecting, and it was just a little disturbing. But was I being unreasonable, expecting him to smile? Was I asking too much? I no longer knew. I just knew that sometimes what you focus on grows.

I always remembered my mother saying, 'Un sorriso non costa niente.' *A smile doesn't cost anything.* And, 'Sorridi e vedrai che tutto passera'. *Smile and you'll see that everything passes.* And during my research into finding strategies to deal with illness, I came across articles about the power of a smile. I didn't send any to Jev, but I tried to gently give him a nudge in that direction, to try and include a little more levity in his days, and to remember that we are more than our illness – or whatever it is that's causing us distress. To be more present, in the moment, as the Eckhart Tolles of this world would say. To always be thinking about his illness couldn't be a good thing.

Of course, it was difficult – the fatigue, the procedures, the pain, the discomfort, it was all unpleasant, and I had no idea exactly how much. But was I asking too much?

I went to work with the image of his scowling face in my mind and it stayed with me through the day. He sent a text telling me he'd arrived safely, and later that afternoon a longer message:

> [J] If you knew what it feels like to be me at the moment, you'd understand how my quality of life has been impacted. Sometimes I can't walk because my ankles are so swollen, and I don't sleep so I have no energy to walk. And when I do manage to fall asleep, I get woken by severe stomach pain and leg cramps. I can't eat sometimes, and there's little I can eat anyway. This is not a way to live. And I want to live, but when I look at other people, I see a strength and a physical well-being that I don't have anymore. Without the transplant I'll never have it again. And without the transplant I won't be around for much longer.

Again, my first thought when I read the message was, *Yes, a sick person's world does shrink.* There was a lot of *me, me, me* in it, and not much about *us*. Even though all that he said was true, I couldn't help but feel that he wasn't taking me into consideration, at all. I didn't like feeling that way, and I even thought that maybe I was lacking in compassion, that I wasn't the good person I thought I was; that it was wrong and selfish of me to want him to consider *us* more, and that asking him to smile more was more about me than him. I wasn't the one facing the prospect of death, the reminder of that reflected in the mirror every single day.

But I knew that just as a sick person can experience a reduced quality of life, so too can a carer. A carer's world shrinks too, but in a different way. Mine did. My life had changed dramatically, and suddenly, as had my relationship with Jev. Getting through my days required a level of effort I'd never experienced before, not even when I was caring for my elderly parents. The co-ordinating and attending medical appointments, the liaising with nurses and doctors, the checking and reminding and providing, it was constant. My needs faded into the background. That's why I felt invisible. He didn't get that. I remember thinking, *I can't lose myself, not a second time.* I'd left my marriage for that exact reason.

Something else bothered me. He made an effort when he was with other people. When his good friend from Queensland visited a little while ago with his wife, he'd made lunch for them and they spent the entire day together. He was exhausted by the end of it, but I remember the photo he sent me. They were all smiling. Yes, Jev sitting between two healthy people, looking ghost-like, and no doubt he saw that too. But he was smiling.

What could I say in reply to his message? I wanted to be able to talk to him about what he was going through, to offer support, and in doing that I wanted it to bring us closer together. But the 'you don't get it' tone of his message didn't encourage that.

I kept it brief:

> [I] I'm sorry, and I understand what you say. I was just hoping to ease your burden in some small way, hoping that I could do that.

I really didn't know what else to say. I didn't want to try and change his mind. I just wanted to see him smile again.

Chapter 18

Jev had the vaccination and, apart from some soreness in his arm, he was feeling fine. It was the day after that that he began to feel other side effects; he had a raised temperature and body aches and fatigue. Whether the fatigue was due to the jab or just the usual, it was hard to tell. He was told that any side effects should go away within a few days, and that he should rest and take Panadol if he had a temperature.

I thought it would be a good idea to check with the transplant coordinator to see if it was okay to be taking the Panadol, as some medications can cause problems in people with cirrhosis. I made the call and let Jev know that paracetamol was safe to take, but not in high doses. And he let me know that he didn't have any. I was a little surprised, as I would have thought that it was something everybody kept in their bathroom cabinet, but not Jev. What to do? He wasn't feeling well enough to go out, so I suggested he call his son who lived nearby and ask him to get some for him. But he was reluctant to do that. I considered calling him myself and asking, but Jev would think that was more micromanaging, and interfering. I then suggested he ask his neighbour, and he said he'd see how he felt in the morning.

The next day he wasn't feeling any better; he still had a temperature. I was working and I couldn't drive to Healesville, but I did consider it. Instead, I called his local pharmacy and they told me that they did home deliveries – all he had to do was place an order over the phone. Easy. I couldn't get through to him until later that day, and again he said he'd call in the morning if he wasn't feeling better.

The next few days were much the same, his temperature still slightly elevated and still the fatigue, but he wasn't spending the days in bed. He was even able to go for a short walk. I suggested going over on the Saturday and taking him some soup and the Panadol, but he said it wasn't necessary, and that I should rest after a busy week at work. I got the feeling that a visit was too much effort for him, that sometimes he just needed to crash. I remember wanting to visit one time after he told me that he'd be spending the day in bed. His response was, 'But what will you do?'

It struck me as an odd question. I didn't need to be doing things, being there with him was surely enough. I thought that he just wanted to be alone. As a person who likes time alone I understood, but I wasn't sure if it was more a matter of him not wanting to be the patient. He never said.

Another reason for not visiting him and taking him the Panadol was that it was Father's Day on the Sunday. His son would be visiting. He didn't think to ask his son to go to the pharmacy on his way, or maybe he didn't want to ask. Again, I wasn't sure.

When I spoke to him early on the Monday morning, he told me that he'd had a rough night. He had severe stomach pain that made him cry out. And he still had a temperature. That didn't sound right, and I thought it was a good idea to let the liver clinic know and see what they recommended. It had been almost a week since his vaccination and he was still experiencing side effects. But he didn't want me to call – he said he'd make the call and let me know. I wasn't sure that it was the right time for him to be taking charge, but I agreed and urged him to do it right away. And what did they say?

'Take the Panadol.'

I called the pharmacy and organised for the Panadol to be delivered, but it wouldn't arrive until later in the afternoon. I let Jev know, and he then sent a message letting me know that he was going back to bed and he'd message when he was up. In other words, 'Don't try and call'. And I didn't, but an hour later I sent:

[I] Are you up?

And then later:

[I] Have you had lunch?

And again:

> [I] Call me when you're up.

It got to 2:00 in the afternoon and I decided to just call, he couldn't, or shouldn't ignore a call. When he answered I knew that all wasn't well: he was slurring his speech, a sign of blood loss. And he sounded confused and anxious. He told me he'd called his son and he was going to bring the Panadol. I knew he needed more than Panadol, he needed to get to hospital right away.

I sent his son an urgent message:

> [I] I just spoke to Jev and he sounds very unwell. I think he needs to get to The Austin emergency department ASAP. Maybe an ambulance needs to be called. Please let me know when you get there.

He called me and let me know that he was on his way over there.

'Thank you. Make sure he takes his phone and the charger and his meds with him. Don't worry about anything else.'

Then I sent another message:

> [I] I've just spoken to the liver transplant clinic and they need to know which emergency department he's taken to so they can follow up. Please let me know what's happening and I'll call the transplant co-ordinator and let her know. I'm very worried. Please call me later. Thank you.

And then I sat and waited; there was nothing else I could do. I wanted to be there but I was an hour away. I couldn't go. It was a reminder of why he needed a support team; if I couldn't be there, someone else had to. And this time it was his son. I was worried, but reassured that he was only a few minutes away. And the closest hospital was only half an hour away – the paramedics would assess him and see how urgently he needed to get there. If he was sent to the Austin I could be there at the same time. That would be easier for me to get to, and he would be where he needed to be, close to the liver clinic.

I sent Jev a message, even though I knew he wouldn't be able to see it, but he would afterwards. The panic I'd heard in his voice … I didn't like it. I wanted to reassure him that all would be well, eventually, as he once said:

> [I] Don't worry, it's all under control. You're probably having another bleed and the hospital will take care of that. Hope to talk to you, and to see you soon. Love you. Xxx

And then I had a thought. He'd had a few bleeds and the transplant unit was concerned at how frequent they were becoming. But they considered him an ideal candidate for a transplant, so maybe this would boost him up the waiting list. Maybe it could be happening sooner than either of us expected. They had said that a liver goes to the sickest person … Jev would surely now qualify as that. Once he'd recovered from this episode, he could be the next to get a call. It was possible, and I was suddenly feeling hopeful.

It was just after 2:30 when his son called. I had my phone beside me as I was Googling frequency of bleeding varices and what it meant, if it could be prevented and how. I was making notes on a pad beside my laptop. I answered the call, and he told me that he was going to put the paramedic on the phone, nothing more. He sounded calm, so I imagined that the paramedic was going to fill me in on what was happening, and which hospital they were going to take Jev to so I could then let the liver clinic know.

I remember what he started to say, and then no more. 'Jev went into cardiac arrest, and we performed CPR but we couldn't revive ...'

I didn't hear another word. I froze.

'No, that can't be. No, no. That's not possible.'

The paramedic was silent. I was in shock, and he knew that. I asked to speak to Jev's son. I needed him to tell me exactly what happened before and after the ambulance arrived. He was there with him, he was the one who could tell me, not the paramedic.

'When I got here, Dad needed to go the toilet so I helped him. I was helping him back to the sofa and he collapsed. I called the ambulance, and I tried to give him CPR. Then the paramedics arrived and took over.' I remember there was no emotion in his voice, his tone was flat.

'How could this have happened? I need to see him. When are they taking him away?'

'They've called the police and they'll be coming soon. And then someone from the coroner's office will come to pick him up.'

'Why the police?'

'A sudden death has to be reported to the police and the coroner's office.'

'Don't let them take him away until I get there, please. I'll let you know when I'm on my way.'

I started calling people to let them know that Jev had died. I had to tell someone, to say the words out loud, to make it seem real. If I told someone it had to be true. I spoke to a couple of friends and they were shocked too, and concerned for me. But I didn't have time for me, I had to get to Healesville. I wasn't sure it was a good idea for me to drive there; I was in no condition to drive, and that's what my good friend Alan called back to say. He lived nearby and he offered to take me.

We drove most of the way in silence. There was nothing to say, and there were no tears. Just a stunned stupor. Travelling along the familiar roads didn't bring the usual sense of anticipation, each landmark signalling that I was getting closer to once again seeing him. I checked my phone and read his final message to me.

One word:

[J] Ok.

I had just let him know that the pharmacy would be delivering the Panadol.

Chapter 19

As we approached the house, we saw the police car parked out the front. They were still there but the paramedics had already gone. Alan pulled up just behind their car. I reached for the door handle but I hesitated. I wasn't here to visit Jev, to sit on the deck with him, to have lunch together. I was here to see his lifeless body. Alan put his hand on my arm and said he'd wait in the car, unless I needed him to go with me. I shook my head and got out of the car.

One of the officers was standing nearby and we spoke briefly. I let him know who I was and he offered his condolences. He was a young man with a kind face. I wondered how often he had to deal with a similar situation; it was part of the job.

I walked down the driveway towards the house. I saw Jev's car under the carport and his boots sitting in their usual spot by the front door. When I opened the door and stepped inside, I saw him lying on the floor just by the door, a towel covering his body and a cushion under his head. I remember thinking that he shouldn't be on the floor. Why had they left him there?

His son was sitting nearby, looking at his phone. He got up when he saw me and we spoke briefly. He told me again what had happened. He then said he'd leave me alone to be with Jev and went outside. No words of sympathy exchanged. I wanted to move towards him and give him a hug, but I sensed that he wouldn't have welcomed that.

I knelt beside Jev's body and looked at his face. His eyes were closed and his mouth was open in an expression of surprise; I knew right away that what happened took him by surprise. A moment of fear as the realisation hit him, and then stillness. I touched his face and noticed bloodstains in his nostrils and in the corners of his mouth, signs of internal bleeding.

I moved the towel and saw that he was naked from the waist down, his long legs lying straight and his hands, his beautiful hands, resting on the floor by his side. I took his hands and placed them in mine, his long fingers unmoving. I looked at them, and again that feeling of familiarity struck me. I saw a life expressed in those hands, *his* life. It wasn't in his face or the words he'd spoken, it was in his hands, a musician's hands. His hands told a story. All hands did. I examined them, compared them to mine; they seemed similar, a masculine version of mine. I traced my fingers over his fingers, over his palms. I followed the creases, looking for something, an indication of the end of his story. I folded his hands carefully across his chest. I leaned forward and kissed his mouth; his lips were still warm. I kissed his forehead and his cheeks. I kissed his hands and rested my head on his chest. I called his name and told him I was there with him. I told him that I loved him. And then I whispered, 'Where are you? Where have you gone?'

What I wanted to do was to lie beside him and to hold him. All I wanted was to be near him. To stay close to him. To hold him and never let go.

I went into the bedroom and took the doona from his bed. I went back and took away the towel and covered him with the doona. I didn't want him to grow cold. I went into the kitchen to get a drink of water. I filled a glass from the tap and stopped to look around the room. I saw an interrupted life. I saw an ordinary day spent doing ordinary things. I saw a cup and saucer on the bench and a teapot sitting beside it. There was his iPad open on the kitchen table and a notebook and pen beside it. The chair had been moved back, as if someone had just got up to put the kettle on to make a cup of tea. The window above the sink was open and there was a breeze moving through the open blinds. There were dishes in the sink waiting to be washed, and a bottle of dishwashing detergent sitting ready nearby. The toaster was out and a loaf of bread was on the chopping board beside it. His pill organiser, with a different compartment for each day and each compartment a different colour, was nearby. I checked and saw that he had taken his meds for that day.

This was where he was, this was what he was doing, this was where he was moving around just a short time ago. This was where his life was suddenly interrupted. Finally interrupted. He hadn't been feeling well, but still he managed to keep his routines going, with a few changes. And the scene in the kitchen was one of those routines; an afternoon cup of tea and a browse on his iPad. The cup was still half-full, he had been sipping his tea when suddenly change was thrust upon him. When he suddenly felt compelled to get up and call his son for help.

It was getting late, and I thought of Alan sitting outside in the car. I really had to leave. I also had to say goodbye to Jev, but I didn't know how to. In Italian culture, wailing was an expression of grief. I remembered visiting a relative in Italy whose mother had died suddenly. She sat rocking back and forth in a chair by her mother's bedside, her arms open wide and crying out loud, very loud.

As I knelt beside Jev's body, I also remembered the dead Indian myna that I once saw by the roadside; it had most likely been hit by a car. Then I saw what must have been its partner appear beside it, screeching madly as if it was saying, 'Get up, get up! It's not safe to stay here. Get up quickly. Let's go! The others are waiting for us. We have to go!' Yes, animals grieve too.

I looked at Jev and that's exactly what I wanted to shout. 'Get up! We have things to do. You can't just lie here, get up. Please get up, now.'

As I looked at his lifeless body, I wanted to wail and rend my clothes, as they did in biblical times. I wanted to express my grief loudly and visibly, as my relative had, and as the myna bird had. But instead, I knelt beside him in stunned silence. I knew this would be the last time I would see his physical form, the last time I would be able to touch him. I knew I would never be able to be in his presence again. And I didn't want that time to end.

I don't remember saying goodbye; I don't remember the words I said. I held his hand one last time, I took it and pressed it against my lips and against my heart, I stroked his face, I kissed his mouth. Then I got up and left.

I had questions I wanted to ask, but the police had gone. I couldn't see Jev's son anywhere and I didn't go looking for him. I didn't want to keep Alan waiting any longer.

But I did have questions. I wanted to know *exactly* what happened. I wanted to know if Jev was already dead when the paramedics arrived. I wanted to know if what happened could have been prevented. Alan said there would most likely be an autopsy and the coroner's report would detail the cause of death.

I knew the cause of death. I knew it was an internal bleed. What I wanted to know was whether anything could have been done to prevent what happened. But I knew that was a question no one would be able to answer.

Chapter 20

As soon as I got home, I called the liver clinic at the hospital and let them know what had happened. I spoke to the transplant coordinator and I remember clearly her shock, and her disappointment. She wasn't expecting that Jev would die waiting for a transplant. She had told me that he was moving up the list. She wanted to see it happen as much as I did. And she liked him, they all did.

She asked me what had happened, and I explained that he'd had a cardiac arrest. She then told me that when he'd called her asking about taking Panadol, she said that if he continued to feel unwell he should come straight back to hospital where they would be able to monitor him properly. That gave me some information I didn't have, because he hadn't told me. If I had known, would the outcome have been different? The 'what ifs' and the 'should haves' kept repeating in my mind. What if I had known? What if I had called the liver clinic myself, as I usually did? What if I had called the ambulance right away? He should have told me, he should have gone back to hospital, and an ambulance should have been called sooner. And I should have seen the signs. I should have.

But we both thought he was experiencing post-vaccination side effects, the hospital too; we were waiting for the Panadol to arrive and for the temperature to subside. We waited too long. But why hadn't he told me what the co-ordinator advised? He clearly didn't want to go back to hospital. Even at the end he was asking for the Panadol. They were his last words to me.

I had to let his colleagues at work know, and his friends. I made calls and I had difficult conversations. His good friend in Queensland thanked me for being part of Jev's life and for being with him during his illness. When I told him that I felt that I could have done more, that I should have been there with him, his words were, 'Stop beating yourself up. Jev talked about you lovingly and he so cherished having you in his life. So, pat yourself on the back instead. You did everything you could. And there was nothing more you could have done – he was dying.'

Those words … I'd never heard them said before, and I'd never thought of Jev as *dying*; the thought had never entered my mind. And I don't think he thought of himself that way either. We both thought he was waiting, waiting for the transplant, waiting for the new life. But he *was* dying. He was slowly dying in front of my eyes.

Later that day, after having dinner alone, I went to bed early. But I couldn't sleep. I kept looking at his framed photo by my bed. I kept waiting for his call or a text message. The phone sat silent on my bedside table. Eventually, I turned it off. I couldn't get the image of him lying on the floor, the expression on his face, out of my head. I was familiar with death, but not sudden death. I was with my mother when she died. I was with her when she took her last breath, I was able to say goodbye. I was leaning over her, talking in her ear, telling her that I was with her and that if it was time for her to go, it was okay, I would be okay. And then there was an intake of breath and no more. It was a gentle death and she didn't die alone. But people do, and in traumatic circumstances. Does that matter? Does it matter how we die? It's still death. I finally fell asleep, thinking of my mother.

Friends started to appear at my door with flowers, cards, and food. They offered support and called me on a regular basis to see how I was going. I hadn't seen Anna and Lucy for our regular catch-ups in a while. I'd been too busy with my carer duties and work. I'd stayed in touch with Lucy and we spoke on the phone often, but not Anna. She seemed to be less sympathetic, and maybe a little too absorbed in her own problems, of which there were a few. Lucy must have let her know about Jev, though; she called to offer her condolences. And then she asked me, 'Were you still in a relationship?'

What? Not the most appropriate thing to ask at the time. But then that was Anna, forthright and not always tactful.

Ian started calling me in the morning; we were both early risers. I would see his name flash across my phone sometimes as early as 6:00, and I was always happy to hear his voice. 'Hi, just calling to see how you're going.' And then we started talking, about the day ahead, about what we were doing, about books we were reading, about our thoughts and feelings. It was a good way to start the day. Before, when the phone rang at that time of the day, it was Jev's name I expected to see; he was the one to call every morning to wish me a good day. But my chats with Ian replaced those for a while. They were the beginning of a new way to begin each day, to begin anew. And I was grateful for that.

Later in the week the senior consultant at the liver clinic reached out wanting to organise a Zoom meeting. He expressed his sadness at Jev's sudden death and was very disappointed that they couldn't get him well enough to have a liver transplant. He was sorry that they couldn't have done more. He told me that Jev was very brave and coped remarkably well with what is an extremely difficult illness. He also said that Jev was a lovely man and that it was a pleasure looking after him; he used to enjoy chatting to him, and he was hoping to see him well again. He also asked for a copy of the coroner's report once it arrived. They wanted to know if they'd missed anything. Like me, they were all probably thinking, *What more could we have done?* He was the kindest man. I also had a chat with Laura, who asked me to stay in touch and to call anytime. Grief counselling was also part of her job.

Everyone's reaction was the same, complete shock and disbelief. Yes, everyone knew he was unwell but they all believed he'd get through. They all wanted him to. I kept having conversations in my head, and sometimes out loud, that I didn't have with Jev when he was alive. I talked to him about the things we couldn't talk about, the things he avoided talking about. I said what was on my mind, frankly and bluntly. I didn't stop to imagine his response, I didn't need to hear him, I needed to be *heard*. I was angry that the end was not the way it should have been, the way we were expecting it to be. But would it have been different if his death had been expected? Would there have been things said, final deathbed words of love and caring and goodbye? I wasn't sure. But one thing I was sure of, one thing I wanted to be different, was the final image he left me with: the scowl on his face when he drove away.

I had to go back to Healesville to collect some of my things. I was a bit hesitant about going, but friends said it would be good to go, good to say a final goodbye to the house where he lived. And I knew that avoiding it would only prolong the disbelief that he was gone, gone for good. I had to go.

When I arrived, Jev's neighbour and friend was working in his front garden. He came over to offer his condolences and he thanked me for being part of Jev's life in his final years. Again, another 'thank you'. I appreciated the acknowledgement, but I was also puzzled. I wondered about the Jev before me – what was he really like? One thing I realised: he was alone.

Wandering around the empty house, empty of *him*, was difficult. I grabbed a few of my things from his wardrobe and, looking at his clothes, I was reminded of how stylish he was – a snappy dresser, as one friend put it. I wanted to feel his presence; I looked for signs, but it was just empty and still, with reminders in every room of a life once lived. I went out on the deck and sat for a while, but I couldn't enjoy the sunshine or the view. Being there without him seemed wrong. I stood and said a final goodbye to the deck, and the view too. I went inside and walked through each room repeating my goodbye. And then I left.

It was a period of lockdown and as I was driving out of the township onto the highway, I heard sirens and saw a police car behind me. I pulled over and rolled down my window. Two female police officers approached my car and one asked me what I was doing in Healesville. They'd obviously checked my number plate and saw that I wasn't a local. I looked at the police officer and burst into tears – the first tears I'd shed since Jev's death. I told her that my partner had recently died and I was visiting his house. Suddenly their expressions changed. They asked me if I was okay and if I had support. They were both so lovely and kind, I cried even more. They told me to take care and wished me well.

When I got back to Fairfield, I stopped at the local supermarket to do some shopping. Standing at the checkout aisle I saw a man walk in and there was an immediate moment of recognition, a little like the one on the railway platform a few years ago. His sallow complexion, his bulging eyes in an emaciated face, his loose pants belted very tight, and his protruding bones through his fleece top, all looked so familiar. And he was wearing a cap. It was as if I was seeing Jev again, as if he was coming in to join me to do the grocery shopping.

He walked past me and I started to breathe again, but something drew me away from the line I was standing in and I followed him. He moved through the aisles with his shoulders slightly hunched. Then he stopped, found what he was looking for and moved on. I stood fixed to the spot, I felt tears coming to my eyes. I was overcome with sadness and surprise. I moved back to the checkout and he was already there, standing ahead of me.

When I left the store, I saw him walking along the footpath, as if he was treading on air. A light, careful step. Just like Jev. I wanted to call out his name, I wanted to see him turn around. I stood and watched as he disappeared down the street. As I had watched him disappear once before.

Chapter 21

Because there was another lockdown it took more than two months to organise the memorial service. After weeks of waiting to see what would happen, it was finally decided that it would have to be an online event. The cremation had already happened and Jev's ashes would be scattered somewhere in a forest by his sons.

It was a Sunday evening and the screen filled with faces as we waited for Jev's son, who lived overseas, to get things started. He introduced himself and spoke for a few minutes about his father, about his love of music and art and his work as a dedicated teacher. A few friends and colleagues spoke and shared memories of their time with Jev. It was good to hear people talk so lovingly about him, even the principal of his school spoke and expressed her respect for Jev, as a teacher and a caring colleague. I was glad that Jev had so many people who loved him and thought highly of him – some I had never heard of – and he would have been pleased with the turnout, maybe even surprised. But as I sat watching the faces on the screen, an uncharitable thought suddenly crossed my mind: *Where were you all when he needed you?*

I didn't speak at the memorial. I didn't know Jev as long as the others had, we didn't have such a shared history, but I felt that I knew Jev in a way they couldn't possibly know, and I couldn't share that with them. The Jev in the last few months of his life was not the person they remembered so fondly.

A friend of his who had moved overseas wrote a very touching tribute and posted it on his online site:

> 'Vale Jev: Colleague, Mentor and Friend
>
> I was told a couple of days ago that one of my closest friends had passed away suddenly. I didn't post or share anything immediately, as I didn't know who knew. Also, I was devastated, too numb to write. And I didn't have the words anyway.
>
> When I started teaching, Jev was my manager (Head of English) and mentor, but we soon became firm friends over a shared love of music, guitars, film, art and books. And, of course, teaching. We spent the next thirteen years at desks alongside each other until I moved to the UK. We talked about all of the above, obviously, but also everything else, including philosophy and spirituality – both of which were a huge part of Jev's life.
>
> We team taught, and supported each other, often falling in with each other's cues instantly when dealing

with students – playing the good cop to the other's bad, the straight man to the other's comedian and so on. Often there would be pop, TV or film references inserted. I almost lost it one day when I was meant to keep a straight face while he was talking to a student. He started gesticulating wildly as he emphasised points. There were others present, but I alone knew he was imitating Gus McCrae, a character from the Lonesome Dove mini-series.

Jev loved to draw. He would attend curriculum (and other) meetings and draw comics and cartoons. When he returned from these meetings, I'd ask how it had gone, and he would show me the cartoons, which was his way of explaining the mood of the meeting without going into details.

Outside of work we ate together, watched films together, listened to music together and, most of the time, just hung out and chatted.

I have lost a great friend. An encourager, supporter, mentor, adviser, confidant.'

The day after the memorial service I was alone at home, no work obligations and no carer obligations and no funeral obligations. No duties remained to fill my day. I didn't have to prepare for work and I didn't have to check my phone to see if Jev had sent me a message, and I didn't have to keep sending him messages to see how he was going. There was a sense of freedom, but I wasn't free of the sadness that followed me around. And I wasn't sure how the two could co-exist.

I was going to have to resume my own life; to continue being a mother, a sister, and a friend. But what was different? I was alone. For the first time since moving into my new home as a single woman, I was alone. Jev had been part of my new life almost from the outset. It's what I imagined I would have experienced had I stayed in the home I'd shared with my husband after the divorce. Too many memories. I wouldn't necessarily be grieving the end of the marriage, but I would be constantly reminded of it.

As I moved from room to room, I felt Jev's absence. As I sat at my computer and looked out the window, I imagined his car coming up the driveway, the key in the door and his voice calling out, 'Hey', as he walked in. I imagined him sitting across from me at the dining table. And there were reminders everywhere; his mug in the kitchen, his cereal in the pantry, his clothes in the wardrobe, his toothbrush in the bathroom, his guitar in the lounge room, his photo on my bedside table. I had to begin the process of removing them, one at a time.

As the days went by, I struggled with the feeling of being alone and, at the same time, the sense of having my life back. Part of me missed him terribly, and part of me felt a weight lifted from my shoulders. Even though I loved him, living with him during the last months of his illness was a challenge, and that was something I couldn't tell anyone. He wasn't the man I had fallen in love with, and the change had happened almost overnight. Had it happened over a protracted period of time it would have been easier to accept, and easier to adjust to. Suddenly Anna's words came back to me: 'You can't really know someone when you don't have to deal with the challenges of life together.' And that's what we had been doing, dealing not with an everyday challenge, but a major life and death challenge.

I felt the need to talk to people, people I didn't know, strangers on the street. If someone smiled at me, I had the urge to stop them and tell them about my loss and ask if they'd ever experienced the loss of a loved one, a partner. And I did exactly that.

I saw Pat walking along the footpath ahead of me – she was an older woman using a walker. I knew instantly that here was someone who would comprehend my pain. I stopped her and we spoke briefly. We both lived in the same street. Then I asked her if she was married. I knew what she would tell me; she had the look of someone who was no longer part of a couple. And that's what she told me. Her husband Bernie had died a few years ago. And then I told her about Jev; we shared our stories.

'I still miss Bernie every day and when I'm sitting on the sofa watching telly at night, I always talk to him, like I used to. I tell him what I'm thinking and I tell him that he shouldn't have left me. You know, I always used to tell him that I wanted to go first, but I didn't. It's not easy being the one left behind, but what can you do?'

Yes, what can you do?

The word 'grief' became part of my vocabulary, a word I didn't know that well. And I was going to need some help to understand it better. After a few days of not knowing how to navigate this new world I found myself in, I spoke to one of the social workers at the hospital and we had a long chat. I started by asking her how often people die waiting for a transplant, and I was surprised to hear that it did happen, often. It wasn't something that came up in the pre-transplant assessment. I asked her if the main carer in most situations was either a husband or a wife. Yes, both but mostly a wife. Were there any that she knew who were in a similar situation to mine, where the relationship wasn't a long-term marriage? No. Did any of those long-term marriages end before the transplant happened? Yes, before and soon after. And what was the feeling after having made the decision to leave? Relief.

She suggested some resources for grief support, including a group that met regularly. But I wasn't ready for that. I did some of my own research and discovered that it wasn't unusual for relationships, marriages, to end when one of the partners developed a life-threatening illness. One study found that in the case of brain cancer, one of the strongest predictors of separation was whether or not the patient was a woman. Men were the ones more likely to leave a sick partner. For some reason, it didn't surprise me.

I had a medical situation of my own while Jev was alive. A routine pap smear picked up some changes in my cervical cells, abnormal changes that required a biopsy. It wasn't an invasive procedure but I would need to have a general anaesthetic, and they preferred it if someone would be with me when I went home. I told Jev, and he reassured me that he would stay overnight with me.

The procedure was booked for October; Jev died in September. As irrational as it seemed, I felt abandoned. When I got home after the procedure, I looked at his photo and asked him, 'Where are you now that I need *you*?'

Chapter 22

I became preoccupied with death and dying. I had experienced the death of my parents, but at an older age both were expected, and I was prepared. Unexpected death is very different, and the grieving process after such a death is different too. It not only takes you by surprise; it brings with it the realisation that life can change in an instant, and that instant can be, as Joan Didion put it so well, an 'ordinary instant'.

In Jev's case, sitting down to a cup of tea in the afternoon. There was no possibility of a bedside goodbye, no last words expressing thanks and love, no final wishes expressed. But what happened was also unexpected for Jev – he wasn't anticipating that his life would end suddenly on the Monday afternoon after Father's Day. The panic in his voice during our last call and the expression of surprise on his face told me that.

He didn't want to go; he wasn't ready to go. He wanted to be well again. To live again. And that's what a transplant would have given him, a 'new lease of life', as he used to say. He had come to realise that the word 'barbaric' that Warren had used to describe organ transplant was not the right word – it was a gift. For someone to decide to be a donor was the most selfless and courageous act, and Jev acknowledged that. Getting to know the staff at the liver clinic, and meeting other people who had either received a new liver or were on the waiting list, made him realise that unless you find yourself in the situation of being either the donor or the recipient, it wasn't something you could fully understand. Awareness was what he had lacked.

I noticed that the news items that caught my attention were all about someone dying, unexpected deaths in particular. The actor Ray Liotta died in his sleep at the age of sixty-seven. The drummer Taylor Hawkins was found dead in his hotel room; he was only fifty. Shane Warne also found dead in his hotel room; he was fifty-two. That's what I took note of, that's what stood out as I scrolled through news items on my phone. Death and dying. I read the obituaries in the newspaper and online. I bought books that dealt with grief and life after loss. A friend called, wanting to tell me about the film she'd just been to see starring Helen Mirren. I wanted to talk about Helen Mirren's stepson, who died at the age of fifty-two.

I was going about my days looking for the presence of death. I was now aware of its sudden appearance, and there was no going back. I looked more closely at people's faces. I looked for signs. And I looked for premonitions. I found a photo Jev had taken of a lunch we had with both our sons.

He'd set his phone up on the table and joined the group, the four of us smiling and waiting for the camera timer to go off. Later when he sent me a copy of the photo, I noticed that he had edited himself out – all that was visible was his arm draped over my shoulder. He said he didn't like the way he looked, his face pale and drawn, his mouth open with a look of surprise. He saw what I would see on the Monday afternoon after Father's Day.

I remembered the time I stood at end of my driveway watching as he slowly walked to the station. I watched him as he disappeared down the street, and a feeling of sadness settled over me. Back in the house, I couldn't get the image out of my mind. He was walking down the street but it felt like he was going away, fading away.

Then there was the afternoon I went walking at the parklands while Jev was resting at home. I saw a black currawong walking beside the path. It was looking for food, but moving slowly. I tried to approach, thinking it would fly away, but it just turned and walked away. I saw it again the next day in the same spot and still searching for food. I knew something wasn't quite right, and I mentioned it to the park ranger on my way home. When I returned a couple of days later, I found it lying dead on the path. Its bright yellow eyes were open and small patches of white were visible at the end of its tail feathers. I gently picked it up and moved it to the base of a tree nearby.

I went on another walk just after Jev's death; it was early morning and it was a bit chilly, so I wore a pair of leather gloves Jev had bought me as a gift. During the walk I took them off and put them in my jacket pocket, something I'd done many times before. When I got back home, I reached into my pocket to take the gloves out and found only one. I'd lost the other one on my walk. It must have fallen out of my pocket. That had never happened before. Where there used to be a pair, there was now only one.

I also started noticing other people, other couples. I kept seeing them everywhere, young and old, all walking hand in hand. One older couple in particular caught my attention. They must have been in their seventies, and I would see them often as they walked along a street near my home. They seemed to move as one, in rhythm. They were always talking and laughing together and holding hands. I remember once stopping my car by the side of the road on an impulse and rushing over to talk to them. I told them that I often saw them walking together and that they always looked so happy. I just wanted to let them know that seeing them always made me feel better. They weren't alarmed by my sudden appearance – an unknown woman rushing across the road to talk to them. Instead, they smiled and seemed pleased. They were more than happy to tell me their story. They were Greek and they had been married for over fifty years and had always lived in the area, in the same house, and they always spent their days together, never apart. They'd had a long happy marriage and they felt blessed, every day.

After I got back in my car, I waved goodbye and watched as they continued their walk holding hands. Was it really a blessing? What would happen if one of them suddenly died? And one day one of them will die and the other will be left alone. How could the other possibly survive alone? A pair suddenly torn apart. A bit like my pair of gloves.

And then there were the written messages I kept coming across, sometimes unexpectedly. I'm not sure where I saw the quote from Seneca, but it came at the right time: 'Every new beginning comes from some other beginning's end.' I had written it in my journal soon after my divorce and came across it after Jev's death. And then I found two entries written over a year apart that reflected the changes in our relationship:

> *Jev is a good presence in my life, a nourishing one. I haven't felt so alive in a long, long time. If I could overcome my attachment to neatness and cleanliness and an oven door that closes properly, without the need for a piece of string, and hot water from the tap that was more than a trickle and renovated spaces, I would be a little more at peace with what is. Like he is. But the disorder and the clutter keep getting in my way. I like aesthetically pleasing spaces. And I don't mean luxurious, just an inviting, comfortable space that feels more like a home. A space that exudes calm and warmth. A space that draws me in. And I want to share that space with Jev. I do. Some of the time. When he says we fit well together, I know what he means, and I know he's right.*

And then this one later on:

> *I need to eliminate stress from my life. Lately there's been too much of it and I notice the negative effects – on my health and my state of being. I can't let Jev's situation get me down. I can't let the changed circumstances disturb me. I'm beginning to think that maybe we connected more on a physical level, not so much on an intellectual or emotional level. I'm*

not sure exactly how compatible we are anymore. Sometimes it feels like there's a huge gap between us, a gulf of separation. But I can't leave now. I will remain a source of support but not sure what will happen afterwards, after the transplant. We'll see. Maybe my relationship with Jev is more, as Anna put it, a weekend relationship. Acknowledging this seems harsh, particularly now, but it's how I feel. And that's important for me to recognise. I can't ignore it. I won't, not again.

Reading the second entry took me by surprise. I couldn't remember writing it and it wasn't how I was feeling after Jev's death – but there *were* moments when things didn't feel right. And I did remember what the social worker had said about long-standing marriages coming to an end, sometimes before the transplant and sometimes after. It did happen.

I also found something Jev had written for his school bulletin about the stresses in education, particularly the remote learning during Covid. He had asked me to read it, to check it, and I'd kept it:

It seems to me that we've all been on a steep learning curve over the last few months and it would be a shame to abandon some of the valuable things we've discovered during that time. 2020 will go down in history as a dark time for all of us but human beings are resilient and inventive and when we eventually move out of this ordeal, it is important to take stock of the few positives and recognise the new growth that has taken place.

It was as if he was speaking to me; the message could apply to my situation. I wasn't quite sure yet what that growth was in my case, but I felt the need to believe that one day I would. The notion of a loved one's death being an opportunity for growth and for a new life seemed hard to accept, but as time went by, I came to see that it was the only way. It was grief with a positive spin, and keeping an optimistic attitude could only be an advantage. To believe that everything works out in the end. To thrive instead of wallowing. To be resilient and not let sadness take over. To accept and keep moving.

That was what the book *Keep Moving* by Maggie Smith suggested, a book she wrote after a difficult divorce. I would let the book fall open at a random page at the beginning of each day and read what it said. It always made me breathe a little easier. It gave me the nudge I needed and the reminder that anything really was possible. I had to keep moving, because there really was no choice, there was no going back.

At the same time, I came across this from Eckhart Tolle:

> 'Some changes look negative on the surface but you will soon realise that space is being created in your life for something new to emerge.'

I wanted to believe that, that a new life was awaiting me, but it was all just words and ideas in books I was reading. I needed to find a way to allow it to happen. To make it work. I couldn't stay stuck in grief.

And then something came my way that I really wasn't expecting. I watched a new Australian series on Binge, *Love Me* starring Hugo Weaving. A series that deals with loss and grief. Hugo Weaving plays the part of the grieving husband, his wife of forty years dying suddenly after long-standing health problems. He had become her carer after a car accident in which she lost a leg, and his days, his *life*, revolved around her needs. What happens next is the surprising, unsettling part. He finds love again only a few short weeks after his wife's death. He was devastated, but also liberated. The realisation he comes to at the end, as do his adult children, is that love and grief can coexist. They get married soon after meeting and his daughter gives a reading at the wedding. She talks about second chances, how they must be sought out and earned. That it requires bravery, and people around us. That even though you're grieving, the next chapter is always waiting for you to start it.

I watched it once, and then I watched it over again right away. It was the most unexpected message; to love again after loss is possible, even right away, because there is no right or wrong time. To keep opening your heart no matter what is not an either/or decision – love can sit well alongside grief. As Ian once said about dealing with a broken heart, 'It's all fuel, and we need fuel.'

The coroner's report finally arrived. And it came with a warning. It suggested that I read it with someone else present, as the content could be distressing. I ignored the warning. I can't remember the details of the autopsy – I didn't focus on the removal of organs, tissue, and fluids – I skimmed through until I reached the cause of death: internal haemorrhaging from oesophageal varices due to cirrhosis of the liver, which led to cardiac arrest. There it was in black and white, and it was what I expected, but still difficult to read. The questions persisted. Could he have survived the heart attack had he been in hospital? Or if the ambulance had been called sooner? I needed to know.

I called and spoke to the transplant coordinator. She answered the phone right away, no need to wait, which was always the case when I'd called in the past. Always available, always ready to talk. She was quick to reassure me that there was nothing I could have done to prevent what happened, and that survival rates after an out-of-hospital heart attack or in-hospital one are usually both poor, and in particular in patients with liver cirrhosis.

Yes, it was helpful to know that, but I also knew that had we not waited days for what we both thought was just an elevated temperature, the outcome could have been very different. Had I been with him, had I been able to see his face, I would have known what to do.

Chapter 23

As the months passed, I noticed the shock of grief starting to diminish. I could think about him, sometimes, without an instant wave of sadness accompanying the thought. And the bitterness of death was starting to subside, it was after all a part of life. An experience that no one could avoid.

I stopped trying to make sense of all that had happened, from my late-life divorce to my experience with *RSVP*, to dating Jev, to his serious illness and unexpected death. I stopped looking for meaning; I stopped looking for a reason why things happened as they did. I stopped asking, 'Why me?' I stopped feeling sorry for myself. And I stopped thinking of grief as a linear process that we have to work through. There was nothing linear or predictable about it. Some days I felt an overwhelming sadness and some days I felt a sense of freedom and possibility. Some days I felt lost and some days I felt that I was exactly where I needed to be. Some days I felt angry at Jev, angry that he'd left me suddenly, that he'd abandoned me, and some days I remembered the good times we had together. Some days I longed for him, for the sound of his voice, for his touch, and some days I relished my newfound solitude. Some days I felt isolated and some days I felt connected to everyone else on the planet. Some days I looked back at what had been and some days I kept my gaze fixed on what lay ahead.

But when I did find myself looking back and thinking of how things weren't so great between us towards the end, I felt a sense of regret that we weren't able to talk things through, that he couldn't. And that even though I tried, I didn't persevere. I only understood after his death that there was a possible reason for his withdrawal. He'd told me about his parents always arguing and that it wasn't a happy marriage. There was never any open display of affection towards each other or towards the children. There were angry outbursts and yelling and threats instead, and often those outbursts were directed at Jev and his sister. I've read that the way we're raised, in particular the relationship between a mother and son, determines the way we conduct our relationships as adults. Being loved and the absence of physical and verbal attacks are crucial factors in being able to develop trust, even in romantic relationships.

Sadly, Jev missed out on that love and support. He struggled at home and his mother eventually threw him out; he came home one day and found his things in a pile outside the house. But he made his way on his own and developed independence earlier than most. I wondered if his upbringing was perhaps the reason he found it difficult to expose his vulnerabilities, to say: 'This is how I'm feeling, this situation sucks and I feel like shit most of the time, and I know things have changed for us, but it won't be forever. We can get through this together. I know we can.' And to acknowledge in some way how I was feeling. Maybe with: 'Hey, I had a shit week, but I get that you're stressed too. I don't want my situation to take its toll on you too, I don't want to burden you. I don't want that. Please tell me if it's all getting too much for you. You need to tell me.'

Sometimes it felt more like a stubborn refusal to express emotion, and sometimes a childlike withdrawal. If only I could have written our dialogue and all we had to do was read it aloud. I did write mine, but it was his that needed to be added.

Sometimes, when in a less charitable mood, I wondered how things would have been if the situation were reversed – if I had been the one needing a main carer and, if after a protracted period of ill health, I had died suddenly. How would Jev have coped with being my carer, working full-time and living in Healesville? And how would he have coped with my death? Would he have grieved for long? I remembered him telling me about the end of his first post-divorce relationship. It had been a year-long relationship and there was even talk of moving in together, which did surprise me after he'd told me that what he felt for her was 'fondness'. It was her decision to end things and it came out of the blue. He wasn't expecting her announcement when she turned up one afternoon to hand back his key.

But did he feel sad afterwards? That's what I wanted to know. And he told me: yes, he felt sad – for a weekend. And within a week or so he was back on *RSVP*, getting on with his life. Not something I would have expected, and neither did she. She soon found him back online and let him know exactly what she thought about that, which only confirmed in his mind that he had made the right decision to move on. Later she got in touch, trying to rekindle the relationship, but he had already started dating again, and with no regrets.

Why did I ask myself these things? Was it to appease a sense of guilt that sometimes crept in, guilt about whether I had done enough to help Jev, or was it simply to see things in black and white? To see the real Jev without grief altering my perception of him, romanticising him. Because that's what people do after a death. And who was the *real* Jev? Unsentimental, restrained, not one to express emotions openly, sometimes aloof and a little critical. Then there was the generous Jev, who gave of his time freely and was always there for a friend or colleague.

I'd heard about post-traumatic stress, but not post-traumatic growth. That was something I came across during my reading about grief. Most studies focussed on the stressful outcomes of a traumatic event, the negative consequences. It wasn't until the late twentieth century that the connection between trauma and personal growth was fully recognised and examined. And the distinction was made between resilience and post-traumatic growth; resilience being the ability to bounce back and deal with stressful events without being overly affected, whereas post-traumatic growth involved positive transformation. The changes that came with the growth included a greater appreciation for life in general and a sense of gratitude for even the smallest things. A shift in priorities and a new understanding of what really matters. A greater understanding of other people's suffering. A greater sense of self, and of personal strength. The realisation that something good is always contained within the suffering, even if it's simply the opportunity for something new. That caught my attention.

The possibility of a changed life, of thriving through adversity and accepting that it's neither good nor bad, filled me with curiosity and anticipation. To know, to *believe* that growth is possible in the space created by loss; and that change, in whatever form, is simply making room for that growth, for something new, was an empowering thing.

In order for that to happen there was one necessary requirement:

Trust.

Chapter 24

Change was something I struggled with when I became a mother. Seeing my son grow and accepting the change that came with that was challenging at times. I looked at the adolescent boy and wondered where the toddler had gone; a toddler with a distinct personality all his own had transformed into someone else. And the bond with that child also alters.

I remember once talking to a parent at my son's school about how quickly our children were growing up, and how quickly our lives were changing. I remember saying, 'I don't like change', and immediately knowing that I shouldn't have uttered those words. I knew that life was constantly evolving, in particular as a parent. Watching my son grow was a reminder of the inevitability of such change. And as other mothers I spoke to acknowledged, it was also a painful reminder that one day they would be adults and our role as a mother would be diminished. There in itself was a loss, the loss of once being a child's main source of support and love. To let go of that, to watch it be replaced, was painful and inevitable.

Getting married also caused me to lose sight of the more adventurous me. As a married woman, I lived a life of routine and stopped taking risks, but during my younger years I was the opposite of that – a risk taker who ran away from home to live a bohemian life in Italy. I had run away from home twice; the first time from my controlling Italian mother and the second time from my husband. It really wasn't too different. Escape – that's what both scenarios required. And boldness, in particular the second time.

I'd spent most of my teenage years wishing and praying that my mother would die. By the age of eighteen I knew that if she were to die, I would have to be the one to kill her. Since I knew that would never happen, my next best option was to run away. There really was no other choice. My mother had a strong constitution and unless there was divine intervention, no sudden illness was going to take her, no sudden death. But I did imagine it – the terminal illness, the chemotherapy, the loss of hair, the swift decline; or even a fatal car crash. In the end I was in too much of a hurry to let life or fate take care of things, so I packed my bags and ran away. And I did have a purpose for my trip.

In my final year at school, we studied D. H. Lawrence's *The Virgin and the Gypsy*; an interesting choice for a Catholic school for girls in the seventies. Reading it at such a young age did have an impact on me, as did watching the film with Franco Nero as the gypsy. Of course, I identified with the young, sexually repressed Yvette, and her struggle to meet family expectations and conform to social norms. The gypsy fortune teller's advice to Yvette was, 'Be braver in your body, or your luck will leave you.' And that's what I had to do.

I remember the afternoon after we'd just watched the film; I was standing outside the school gates waiting for the bus. I looked at the other girls around me, wearing their buttoned-up blazers and their gloves and hats, and I knew that I had to leave. And I had to have a plan. After finishing school, I started an Arts degree at university but I deferred my studies and found a job as a clerk with the public service instead. I saved my money, and then I left.

I packed my things and left Doncaster – a cultural wasteland, as I once heard it described – and my repressed upbringing, before my luck left me. I went in search of my own gypsy, and like Yvette, I wanted to fall awfully in love. It was an escape, but also a pilgrimage. I wanted to visit Keats's grave in Rome. He was part of the reading I did for my first-year subject at Monash University, Romantic and Victorian Literature. It was his poetry in particular that stayed with me, and that I took with me to Italy. I went in search of my gypsy and beauty. As Keats wrote:

> 'Beauty is truth, truth beauty – that is all
> Ye know on earth, and all ye need to know.'

I found myself alone in a foreign country at the age of twenty, living from day to day without the comfort of security. And the people I met in Italy were outside my convent girls school experience of life. I met a gentle anarchist who idolised Che

Guevara, a frustrated artist who had attempted suicide, a public servant who read Hemingway and Charles Bukowski obsessively, a drug user who wrote poetry, a married newspaper editor who was a serial adulterer, a married businessman who declared his love for me, a beautiful young man named Fortunato who wore jeans with colourful knee patches and made heads turn everywhere he went, two odd sisters, Marisa and Floriana, who ran a 'Scuola Interpreti' for locals wanting to learn English, and a journalist who bragged about his contacts and the size of his penis. It was indeed a very different experience.

That's where I met him, my gypsy. Nothing afterwards compared. Our first meeting was one evening when he rang the doorbell of the apartment I was sharing with Fiona, another woman who taught English at the Scuola Interpreti. When I opened the upstairs window and looked down, I saw him casually leaning back against the wall of the opposite building with his leg bent back and his foot resting on the wall. He had his hands in his pockets and he looked up at me with a grin. He was looking for his friend, who was dating Fiona. I told him they weren't home and that I'd let him know he'd come by. He suggested coming up and waiting for them to come back, but I wasn't sure that was a good idea, and I had evening classes to get to after dinner. I stood at the window watching as he walked away. I thought about the way he looked at me, with a 'naked suggestion of desire', the way the gypsy had looked at Yvette. It wasn't long after that meeting that he became my boyfriend.

How could I begin to describe Maurizio? He was unique. He was larger than life. He was magnetic. He was fearless.

He was fun. He was charismatic and charming. People were drawn to him. Everywhere we went people would notice him, women in particular. When we walked along the corso taking our passeggiata, an Italian custom in the evening to go out walking and socialising, we would constantly be stopped by people who knew him, men and women wanting to talk to him; the women reaching out to touch him, his arm, his face. Everyone wanted to be his friend. He had a childlike wonder that he never lost, and he was able to make a walk to the local café a great adventure. He was also a hopeless romantic and a drug user, and without a steady income that led to a few potentially perilous adventures. But it was the most interesting and thrilling time of my life. There was no fear, even in the most challenging moments, instead there was something thrilling about living on the edge.

I later found a letter I had written to my sister back in Australia, telling her about my life with Maurizio:

> *When you say that your life lacks intensity over there, I know exactly what you mean. You see, these past few months with Maurizio would be impossible to duplicate over there. I told you that Maurizio had managed to find a car that he could afford to buy, well, some evenings when money is running short, we have to drive around parking lots under the cover of darkness and pump petrol out of other cars – occasionally getting cigarettes and loose change etc into the bargain. I know, a life of petty crime doesn't sound ideal, and certainly not what a Catholic girls school education prepared me for, but with Maurizio*

it doesn't feel quite so wrong. Although, I have to say, I'm not sure we can go on like this forever. Something has to change. And I sometimes ask myself if coming back to Australia might be the best thing, for a while at least. What would you do in my situation? Before you answer remember that I have had other relationships in my time here and Maurizio is the only one who has made me feel safe, yes, an odd word to use considering how uncertain our situation is. But he's never afraid and I admire that. He's the sort of person who is capable of making the most of any situation. He has incredible incentive and I've discovered just how intelligent he is. People are in awe of him and say that he is a very cultured man. But he is also what you might call a professional thief, without a regular job he always manages to survive somehow. It's living in the most real sense of the word and there is nothing ordinary about him. If I told you about all the things that have happened, all the various 'adventures', I'd be writing a book. Who knows, perhaps I will one day.

I think the first time I knew that Maurizio was one of a kind, *really* knew, was during a walk in a forest. We were walking and talking, and he would stop occasionally to look up at the trees and the clear blue sky. At one point he bent down and picked something that was growing alongside the path. And then he handed it to me: a four-leaf clover. I remember taking it with a feeling of astonishment. How did he do that? How many times had I searched for one, desperately sifting through the clover in my garden at home, searching for my good luck charm? He didn't say anything, he just smiled. I still have it, pressed between the pages of Katherine Mansfield's journal, a book I carried with me during my travels in Italy. She had lived her own bohemian life, and the last two years of her life in Italy.

They certainly were different times. Yes, I was younger. Yes, most of us live fearlessly when we're young. And yes, that period too would have ended, as it did. Maurizio and I had talked about him coming to Australia, but with his criminal record he wouldn't be given a visa or passport. As it turned out, it didn't matter. He had been on parole for drug offences and after breaching his parole conditions he went back to jail. I found myself living alone and with only sporadic work teaching English to Italian businessmen, so I decided to go back home to Australia and complete my university degree, something I had interrupted when I ran away.

Removed from the intensity of life with Maurizio, I suddenly found myself questioning whether living that way could be sustained. Whether a life with Maurizio, who had no idea of his own limitations, would be one of constant uncertainty and struggle. I didn't know that I could deal with that. I reached out to a friend in Italy, a retired teacher who had taken Maurizio under her wing. The friend, Altera, saw something in him, some potential, and she tried to help him as best she could. When I wrote to her telling her that I was having doubts about coming back and resuming a life with Maurizio, she understood and she encouraged me to continue my studies and to forget him. I still have her letter; it was letters and phone calls in those days.

Your love for Maurizio was a great love, generous and supportive, but he would have destroyed you, and forgive me if I speak so harshly. With all his power of imagination and his sense of living in absolute freedom, he is incapable of living in reality with all the responsibilities and limits that reality can impose. We can, in fact we should, keep the drawer to our dreams open, woe if we didn't. And in general, it is possible to live in harmony with the demands of the real world and our dreams. The quotidian and the ideal, the two can help each other along.

She understood my decision, but Maurizio didn't. He said this in a letter, which also came with a poem he'd written for me:

Wherever you may be and go, know that I won't have peace until you explain your decision to me face-to-face. I need to see your face, look into your eyes and hear your voice. I won't be stopped by visas or passports, and you will have to at the very least explain your behaviour and your silence. I love you like never before, Ida. Don't forget this. I can only tell you how much I miss you, and that is atrocious.

I carried his letter with me, and the poem, and I read them over and over again. But Altera was right – I had to forget him. I put them away in a box with all the other letters he had written me. I put the box at the back of my wardrobe and tried not to look back.

I finished my studies and started looking for a job. And then I did something very ordinary – I got married. Once married, I lived a conventional life that I would never have imagined possible. There was predictability, responsibility, and accountability. All things I had avoided for a long time. But I wasn't sure it was possible to live a life without those things. Then I read the poems of Jack Gilbert and I was reminded that it was indeed possible. It was possible to live a life not based on security and material possessions. He did. He never owned a house, not even a car. He didn't think you could see anything from a car because it was moving too fast. And that's how we sometimes move through life, too fast.

After my divorce, I imagined going back to Italy. I imagined being reunited with Maurizio. I imagined us running into each other in Piazza della Signoria in Florence; it was a place we visited often, and the Uffizi gallery too. I imagined that first moment of recognition. I imagined his smile, not of surprise but of knowingness. And I imagined what he would say:

'Finally, Ida, you have come back to me.'

But I couldn't go back to him; I couldn't because he was dead. I'd heard the news from a friend, but I didn't know exactly what had happened. He mentioned travel to Africa and an illness, nothing more.

Chapter 25

*J*ust as Jev had an interest in alternative healing practices, he also had an interest in the mystical, the afterlife, and mediums. He once told me about his experience with a medium, one he'd never forgotten. It involved one of his students, Jake. When Jev was on Bus Duty after school, Jake would always be sitting in the bus shelter, and he'd always take a packet of two-minute noodles out of his bag. He would tear the bag open and sprinkle the flavoured powder on the block of noodles and then start munching it as if it was some sort of biscuit. They would always have a laugh about it. Jev started calling him Noodle Man after that, and Jake laughed about that too. But he was a troubled student. One night he got drunk and stoned, and ran the stolen car he was driving into a tree. He was only sixteen and he was killed instantly.

Jev always thought that if he'd survived the crash, with the right guidance he could have ended up okay. When he went to see a medium, she relayed a few messages about his personal life and then told him there was a kid who wanted to let him know that everything was okay, that all was good. And that he always appreciated Jev's support, that he enjoyed their chats. That took Jev by surprise. He hadn't been thinking about Jake, at all.

And so I decided that's what I would do: I would see a medium too. I was hoping for some message from the afterlife; he was a believer, after all. I had expected something from him, but months had passed in silence. In all that time I didn't even have a dream about him. There was one moment when I thought it was Jev sending a message. I was driving the car only days after his death, and as soon as I turned the radio on, I heard Willie Nelson singing 'You Were Always on My Mind'. The lyrics brought tears to my eyes. It was as if Jev was apologising and acknowledging. And then I found myself sobbing. I was looking for a sign – a song, of course it would be a song.

I asked a friend who'd had some experience with mediums to recommend someone. I made an appointment for a reading and waited for the call. It was still during Covid and even though we were out of lockdown, people were still slow to resume normal activities, and still wearing masks. I figured a phone reading would probably work better, as the masks tended to muffle voices and I would probably find it hard to understand what he was saying. The whole session would be spent saying 'Pardon?' and having to repeat everything. That's what I found happening in the classroom and when out talking to people. I also thought that a reading without seeing someone might even be more telling; he wouldn't be able to read my body language. Nonverbal cues can sometimes reveal more than words do.

He called and we spoke for a bit, and he asked me who I wanted to connect with. I told him what had happened, that Jev had died suddenly, but I didn't give any specific details. He did want to know Jev's date of birth and the date of his death, but nothing more. I waited while he tried to make contact with him. After a few minutes of silence, he told me Jev was there, but he wasn't coming through clearly. He was still in the period of transition, which could last months. He told me that he had guides around him and they were helping him review his life on Earth; to see what had happened and what decisions he'd made, and perhaps how he could have done things differently. He had left this life suddenly and he wasn't ready to go, and that was something he was struggling with. The medium stopped again to try and see if there was a message coming from Jev – he didn't say anything out loud, it was a silent communication.

Meanwhile, I thought about what he'd said. I could imagine Jev on his new journey. I could imagine him going on that new journey with a sense of awe and wonder, wherever it led. It would be a new adventure that he would waste no time exploring.

After a few more minutes, the medium said he had a clear message for me from Jev. I found myself sitting upright and listening attentively.

'He says to forget him. His exact words are: "Forget me. I'm not worth stopping your life for the rest of your life. Time is precious, remember that."'

That was it. One brief message, telling me to let him go. To get on with my life. To stop feeling sad. That he wasn't worth it. That took me by surprise ... and then maybe not.

When I later told a friend, she was a little sceptical. It's not that she didn't believe in the possibility of an afterlife or communicating with the dead. She didn't think it was something someone in the spirit world would say; that Jev would say. She thought it was a bit harsh. At first, I agreed with her. I could see her point – there was nothing there for *me*. No words of comfort. No words of love. And that's what I was hoping for. I was hoping to hear him say something about us, about our time together, and maybe even acknowledgement of what I had done for him, that he appreciated it. Something that would help ease my regrets.

Whether it was really coming from Jev or it was the medium trying to make me feel better, I didn't really care. Just to have the words spoken, to have my feelings acknowledged, would have been enough. The things I'd wanted when he was alive.

Later that night, I thought more about it and it struck me that it did sound like something Jev would say. No sentimentality, no ambiguous messages, no bullshit. That was Jev, blunt and to the point, and sometimes a little too much that way. 'Forget me and move on.' It's what he would have wanted me to do. It's what he would have done.

Then I thought about that night in bed after we'd made love. His words came back to me: 'It's only circumstances, and circumstances change.' At the time I couldn't understand why he'd said it. But thinking back to that night after seeing the medium, his words seemed almost prophetic.

Chapter 26

I'd been sitting at home alone reading books about grief and loss: *The Other Side of Sadness, The After Grief, On Grief and Grieving, Finding Meaning, Bearing the Unbearable, When Breath Becomes Air*. It was time to do something; I was *ready* to do something.

I'd heard about people taking solo journeys, sometimes after a loss, and sometimes for no reason, and it was always a transformative experience. Robyn Davidson went on a 2700km trek across the Australian desert with just her dog and four camels. She never gave a specific reason for deciding to go on her trek, but it did become a journey of discovery. Cheryl Strayed took a similar journey of self-discovery when she went on a solo hike along the Pacific Crest Trail not long after her mother's sudden death, and she had no prior hiking experience. Raynor Winn and her husband Moth decided to walk the South West Coast Path after losing their home, and after he was diagnosed with a terminal illness. They lived and camped out in the wild, carrying just their rucksacks with a few of their possessions. She was fifty and he was fifty-three.

I knew I wasn't going to trek across the desert or go on a hike or climb a mountain. But I'd had enough of sitting at home reading books about grief and loss. I had to start moving again. So, what did I do? I went on a solo walk along the Spiritual Healing Trail at the Darebin Parklands. No dog or camel or partner for company, or need to pack provisions or cooking equipment or a tent. Just a good pair of walking shoes, a bottle of water, a sense of curiosity, and a map. I always struggled with directions, even when they were coming from my car navigation system. Getting lost was always my fear.

I was once driving along the Monash Freeway on my way home after a day of casual work; it was an unfamiliar road, but I'd had no trouble getting there in the morning. For some reason I missed a turn-off that would have taken me back home and found myself on the way to Phillip Island instead. I panicked for a few minutes and then seriously considered continuing and spending the weekend at Phillip Island. It was a Friday afternoon; it was tempting, and it would have been the first spontaneous thing I'd done in a long time. A *very* long time. A weekend alone, away from family and obligations, wasn't something I'd ever contemplated. Maybe it was the universe giving me a nudge. But I eventually found the off-ramp and made my way back home.

On my last walk at the parklands, I picked up a brochure about the Spiritual Healing Trail on display outside the ranger's office. I went home and started reading. I was immediately captivated. I'd walked at the parklands often, even with Jev, but I'd never known the trail existed. It was created by the local Aboriginal community as a gift for all who visited the parklands and as a gesture of reconciliation. And I knew nothing about Aboriginal mythology. I learnt that Darebin Creek and the surrounding land was created by Bunjil, an ancestral being and a deity. He was the one responsible for creating the rivers, bushland, flora, and fauna. His intention was to bring joy and peace and healing to everyone who walked there. Being at the parklands was always a peaceful experience, but to think of it as a place of healing was something new to me, and it was what I was in need of.

The aim of the Spiritual Healing Trail is to help people improve their emotional and spiritual well-being through a sense of connection with the land. The brochure suggested picking up a gum leaf at the start of the trail to carry along the way, and to keep it afterwards as a 'link to the spirit of the land.' So, that's what I did. With a backpack, the brochure, and a gum leaf in hand, I started my journey; a journey into the 'realm of nature and possibilities.'

I set off early one morning just after sunrise, as there wouldn't be too many people about at that time. Following the map, I started to travel the 1.4km trail, stopping at a series of markers along the way; each one noting a stage along the journey. There were five in all. There was also a plaque honouring the memory of Aboriginal elder Reginald Amos Blow, better known as Uncle Reg, a man 'of wisdom who believed this land should be used for healing of all people.'

An Interrupted Life

> 1. Gathering: Gather your thoughts. Identify and prioritise your issues.

The first marker was set in a peaceful spot off the track. I sat on the ground beside it and read the instructions in the brochure. In order to continue the journey, I had to be clear on which issues I had control over and those I didn't. That wasn't too difficult. What I was grappling with were feelings of loss and grief and regret, and I had control over that. As much of my reading told me, how we feel about something, how we respond to the events in our life, good or bad, is a choice. I had come to understand that more as time went on. What I had no control over was how my future would play out. That was something I had to let go of; worrying about what might be, as well as what might have been.

> 2. Purifying: Let the water wash away issues you have no control over.

I crossed the creek and stopped at the bank to let the water wash over my hands and carry away the issues I had no control over. A symbolic *letting go*. To add to the feeling of release, I picked up a twig that had fallen from a nearby tree and dropped it into the creek. I watched as it disappeared, carried away by the running water. I took a deep breath and moved on.

> 3. Contemplation: Draw energy from the good things in your life.

The third marker was beside a bench overlooking a small pond where a few ducks were swimming, occasionally dipping their heads under the water as they searched for food. I sat on the bench in the morning sun and began thinking about what I had learnt from the recent events in my life, and the positive values that came from this. I recognised that gratitude was something to be valued, and to be expressed. I had experienced a sad loss, but in that loss there was also an opportunity for something good to come, for acceptance and growth.

> 4. Possibilities: One step at a time.

I continued walking along the edge of the creek until I came to another crossing. There was a fish ladder to help the fish migrate up and down the creek, bypassing the obstacles in their way. For the traveller, the ladder symbolised the necessity to take one step at a time when overcoming problems.

> 5. Ready to Go: You're on top of the world and on top of your issues.

I followed the trail across the creek. There was a hill ahead and I slowly made my way up it. It wasn't an easy climb, and I had to carefully watch my footing along the way, I didn't want to stumble and fall. Just as the brochure said, it takes effort to reach a goal.

Once I reached the top I stood and looked around. There were views of city buildings on one side, and trees and hills on the other. It was the first time I'd been there, and it really felt as though I was on top of the world, and ready to go. The brochure said to 'make a declaration to yourself to realise in both word and action whatever you have identified during your journey.' I stretched out my arms in the morning sun and silently declared that the past was over, I couldn't go back, I couldn't alter what had been. I would stop feeling sorry and sad and disappointed. I was grateful for all that had been, for my time with Jev. I was now ready for whatever the future might bring. I was opening my arms to a new life – I was welcoming it in.

As I walked down the hill, I felt lighter. I crossed over the wooden bridge and walked past the sculpture of what looked like a giant egg, but the brochure told me it was called The Nest. I then found myself in the middle of an open grassy plain with ducks and other waterfowl wandering about. I sat on a nearby log. My journey along the spiritual trail had ended, but another one was about to begin.

As I walked back to my car, I thought about the question Jev had asked me when we first started seeing each other, 'What do you want?'

I had read him Jack Gilbert's poem; I wanted to fall in love again, one last time. And I did. But at the time I didn't think too much beyond that line. It was only afterwards that I came to fully understand the rest of the stanza.

Chapter 27

After going on the Spiritual Healing Trail, my walks at the parklands changed. They were no longer just walks, or just an exercise routine. I started to notice things more; the trees, in particular. But more than that, I felt a sense of connection to the place, or as the brochure put it, a 'link to the spirit of the land.' I wasn't just in nature, surrounded by trees and flora and fauna – I felt immersed in it. I still had the gum leaf that symbolised that link; it was sitting on my bedside table where I could see it every morning and evening.

I continued my walks almost every morning, and I came to know the trees and the shrubs – not just by their names. I came to know them as you would a friend, and they me; well, that's how it felt. The leaves brushing against me, or a twig from one of the shrubs gently poking me as I walked past, as if they were saying, 'Hello, again.' It always took me by surprise. I thought of them as my arboreal friends, and like good friends they were always there for me. I could always rely on them. They never leave. I started to feel a bond, both physical and emotional, and it felt reciprocal. Walking past, I brushed my hands along the leaves of the trees, and I can't quite explain how, but I felt a sense of recognition. They knew who I was, that I was on my morning walk. They were expecting me. They sensed me coming. They welcomed me.

And they heard me. I was very good at soliloquies when I was walking at the parklands. I would have conversations with myself and speak out loud. If Shakespeare could have heard me, he'd be taking notes. I think it was the government's Covid mask-wearing mandate that got me started, that made it easier to do. I would be out shopping and wearing a mask, and I could speak my thoughts out loud with no one noticing. It slowly became a habit.

There's a river red gum that stands beside the walking path. Most people walk or jog or cycle past it. I stop. I stop and look up. Over time, I noticed people looking at me as my gaze was turned upwards. Then they noticed the tree.

It's a majestic tree with twisted limbs growing in all directions. It has a real presence, and every time I have to step up close and run my hand along its smooth bark. Sometimes someone will look up too and smile, then we acknowledge what a splendid thing it is. I've had a few encounters with fellow walkers under that tree; that too has been an added change to my walks, another positive change. I've made what I call 'parklands friends'.

A group of sheoaks grow along the creek bank. I always used to walk past them. One day I left the path and walked through an opening nearby. I immediately felt as though I was walking into a room full of friends, female friends. They were positioned close together and as I walked through, I could reach out and touch one on either side of me. The slender needles brushed against my face and arms as I wandered along. I noticed that one was leaning away, bent but still growing upwards, and then I saw why. It was giving the sheoak beside it room to grow.

Sometimes when the wind was blowing, I could hear a distinct sound coming from the trees, like whispering voices. I thought to myself, *They're talking*, or as Henry Lawson asks in his poem, 'Why are the sheoaks forever sighing?'

One tree in particular stands out; it's a palm tree that sits solitary next to a narrow track along the creek. It leans towards the water. I always made the detour to visit it, to stand beneath it and rest my hands along its spiky bark and let the long fronds drape around me. Emerging from the track on my way back to the main path, there were a few overhanging branches and shrubs that I had to make my way around. There again, I would be greeted with a gentle prod. It always happened as I was leaving.

And then there was the olive tree that I came across by chance. There were several growing around the parklands, but this one was almost hidden in a more secluded spot. It sat on a small rise, and its gnarled trunk spread out in all directions. One of its thick branches that obstructed the track had been cut back, and around the remaining stump new growth could be seen; small branches were starting to grow from it. I ran my palm along the smooth stump and the new branches. It reminded me that growth really can come from loss. The tree wasn't stunted from the loss of a limb; it continued to grow. Walking past it every day became my reminder to let go of loss, of sadness, and to let life in. To remember that loss is the threshold to change, and that change is something to embrace, in whatever form it comes.

When I told Ian about my tree friends, I didn't have to explain. He gave me a nod of shared understanding and said, 'Trees are people to me.' He spends quite a bit of time at his bush property in NSW where he's surrounded by nature, and he refers to the place as his spiritual homeland. He gave me a book to read, *The Hidden Life of Trees* by Peter Wohlleben. In it, Wohlleben writes about trees as social beings – they live in a social network made up of families, including children and parents. And they communicate with each other via a network of roots beneath the ground and the branches above. I had seen signs of these interactions as I walked through the parklands, it was happening everywhere. The roots of the huge gum trees were visible above the ground, and they spread in all directions, intersecting with the roots of neighbouring trees. Connecting one to the other in what looked like an act of friendship. I saw other signs of friendship, of kindness – where fallen branches, and sometimes entire trees, didn't land on the ground, they fell in between the branches of a nearby tree as if being held in the arms of a friend. As if in a loving embrace.

Chapter 28

Just as I began connecting with nature, I noticed connections with people happening too; brief moments of connection. It started with the man on his bike who always called out, 'Have a happy Monday', or whatever day it was, as he whizzed by. The first time I was so surprised I didn't know how to respond. But after that, every time he called out I would reply with a, 'Thank you, and you too.' He would turn and smile.

After a while, we began to recognise each other and he would always follow his greeting with a huge smile and a wave of his hand. Our paths crossed for just a few seconds but seeing him, hearing his voice call out to me, set the tone for the rest of the day. It was enough to make me feel uplifted, almost for the rest of the day.

But there were others. Helen, who walked her dog Romy, and Mary who walked Kovu, and the older gentleman with a Papillon, named for its butterfly-like ears, who he had named

Rocky. That made me smile; such a small thing named after the boxer played by Sylvester Stallone. He told me that he'd considered the name Brutus but didn't think he had any assassin in him. That made me smile even more.

Then came John, someone I ran into walking up the bluestone steps, all eighty of them. Some people jogged up, and that's what he did. Jogging up the steps was a cardio workout for them. I struggled to walk up once without stopping – and then there was John who would jog up and down, several times. That's how we got talking. I discovered that he also had an Italian background; our conversations then became a mixture of English and Italian.

Julie was my age. We would often cross paths on our walks, and on one occasion we acknowledged each other with a smile and started talking. From then on, we met on a regular basis and walked together. It was never planned, but still it became a regular thing. We had both lost a partner recently, although in different circumstances, and after a few walks we found we had so much more in common – we had almost parallel lives. It was the strangest thing, our shared experiences. We seemed to plunge right in, talking about all the difficult aspects of our personal lives without hesitating.

'Do you ever feel lonely?' I asked her.

'I was thinking about that on the weekend. My daughter stayed over at her boyfriend's and I was at home alone for the whole weekend. I didn't have any plans and I was feeling a little uncomfortable, and a little anxious, about being alone. But I'm not sure if that's the same as lonely. That's what I was asking myself.'

'Well, alone and lonely are different things. I'm aware of being alone too. And living alone at a later age in life sometimes makes me feel vulnerable.'

'How so?'

'Being alone and unwell. That's what makes me feel vulnerable, especially now that we're living in a Covid world. I think that's what's made me start thinking about it more, that and Jev's illness.'

'You're pretty fit and healthy, you don't have to worry about that. But if that's ever the case, you have people around you that you can call on, and that includes me.'

Reassuring Julie, she always said the right thing. It was as if we were long-time friends who had been together through all the ups and downs of life. Running into her and having our walk and talk was always an enriching experience.

It really was a strange thing. I ran into these people almost always at the same place and almost the same time. We didn't organise to meet, it was always a spontaneous thing, but I looked forward to seeing them, I *knew* I would be seeing them. They were sometimes brief exchanges, sometimes a little more in-depth. We were strangers who found ourselves talking about all manner of things. What they say about revealing things to strangers that we couldn't do with anyone else was true at the parklands. And yet, it felt natural, it didn't feel odd, and it didn't feel inappropriate. There was real connection. Maybe that had something to do with the spirit of the place. Sometimes it was just a smile exchanged with a passer-by, but that smile lingered and lifted my mood. They say humans are social beings and that social interaction is crucial to well-being. Well, even a few minutes of interaction at the parklands could provide that.

There were also the chance encounters, the one-off meetings. Walking down the bluestone steps, I passed a young girl and boy sitting halfway down and smoking. They looked like teenagers, and the familiar scent of dope that was wafting around them told me that they probably were sharing a joint.

'That's a familiar smell,' I said.

I could see from the frown forming on the boy's face, that he was expecting a reprimand. Instead, I said, 'Ah, once upon a time.'

The frown disappeared. He looked at me and nodded knowingly, 'Once upon a time'.

I inhaled deeply and continued down the steps.

Peter and I ran into each other occasionally and it always surprised me that he remembered my name. It was always, 'Good morning, Ida.'

Once he followed it with, 'How are you today?'

It wasn't too long after Jev's death and my reply was, 'Some days are better than others.'

He stopped to look at me and said, 'We're walking here in this amazing place. Have to remember, life is good.' A reminder that I carried with me for the rest of the day.

The next time I saw him, I said, 'Peter, we're both brave to be out here this morning. It's so cold.'

'Not after you've been walking for a while. And the wattle is in bloom, it's yellow blossoms everywhere you look.'

Yes, another timely reminder to be present and grateful.

There was one man who walked his son to school. He had the most beautiful open smile. It was heart-warming. One morning he was walking alone, and he was wearing a suit and carrying a briefcase. We smiled at each other and I said, 'That's not your usual look.'

He laughed and his face lit up even more, 'No, but I do sometimes have to go into the office.'

I saw him just a couple of days later, again wearing a suit. I pointed at him and said, 'What, again? Another day in the office?'

His open smile appeared right away. And then he stopped to say hello and ask my name, and he told me his, Matt. I couldn't resist, I told him he had a beautiful smile, and again his face lit up. He said, 'Maybe if you saw me at the other end of the day it might be different. After a day at the office, not so happy.'

'I'm not sure I believe that. But I might have to switch my walk to the end of the day and see it that's true.'

His smile, still there. 'No, you're right, it's not true.'

'I'm glad to hear that. And are you always punctual when you're on your walks here?'

'When it's a work in the office day I have to be. I have to catch the 8:00 train.'

'Hmm, I'm going to have to make an effort to be punctual too then. I might get to have a regular dose of your smile.'

He started laughing. Another connection made.

One morning I was standing off the track under a gum tree. It had low-hanging branches that made it possible for me to stroke it and wrap my arms around it, and sometimes I would rest my cheek on its smooth bark. It was a more physical way of saying hello, and getting a rush of oxytocin. I noticed some deep cracks along the trunk, like scars after a wound. I ran my fingers along the cracks, and it was as though the tree had had its share of pain too, but remained resilient and strong. Being there was soothing and calming, and for a few moments I was fully aware of my surroundings. I was enveloped by the energy of nature and I was invigorated by it. I'd read somewhere that interacting with a tree, through forest bathing and tree hugging, did increase feel-good hormones. I always went off the main path to do this as I knew there would be a few raised eyebrows from passers-by if they saw me.

I didn't hear the woman walking her small dog along the track, but her dog saw me and pulled on the lead to get over the shrubs to reach me. I said hello to the woman and patted her Chihuahua, which seemed excited to see me. She then said, 'He doesn't normally like people.' That also made my day.

Sometimes I catch snippets of conversation and think, *I'd like to hear more of that.* On one walk I heard two young joggers talking earnestly about something. As they jogged past me, I caught one of them pose the question, 'Ten per cent of NATO'S budget or Germany's?' I didn't hear the answer. It wasn't particularly a topic I would be interested in, but it intrigued me that a young couple would be discussing something of the sort while they were jogging. Further along my walk I saw them again; this time they were walking in my direction. It was a sunny morning and I was in a light-hearted mood, so as they approached I said, 'I have to ask – which was it? NATO or Germany?'

They both stopped and we all had a laugh. Then they told me they were talking about the war. It didn't require any elaboration. It was a moment, a shared moment.

I realised that my dose of human contact at the parklands, brief as it was, sustained me in a way I would never have imagined. I forgot my sadness, my loss. If Uncle Reg were still alive, I'd tell him that the parklands truly *is* a healing place.

Chapter 29

I've read that people sometimes hold on to sadness because they become so well-acquainted with it; they know it so well it becomes a habit. But I can't do that.

I've recently discovered something about myself – sadness doesn't suit me and I can't accommodate it, even if it visits only for a short while. I can't wear it like a familiar coat that I can put on and take off, and it's not a fog I can dance in and out of. No, sadness constricts me, like wearing armour. It stifles me. It brushes against me with jagged claws and if I let it, it holds me captive. I find myself holding my breath. My chest tightens and by body stiffens. My face becomes fixed and I can't smile. And that's not who I am; I like to smile, and I like to see other people smile. I like the sound of laughter, mine and other people's. And I want to laugh again. I know that now.

It's been almost a year since Jev died, and I've removed every reminder of his presence in my house: the framed photos, the books, the clothes, the drawings, the maple syrup in the pantry, the guitar. Ian suggested I keep one of his drawings as a *memento mori*. I tried. I put one up on the wall, but every time I caught sight of it I felt a wave of sadness, a tightening in my chest. I had to take it down.

I finally took all his things and donated them to the op shop, the one we would often visit. I know that I have to keep moving, and those things were stopping me from doing that, they were holding me back. They were a constant physical reminder of his absence in my life. And I had to let go.

I'd kept some of his ashes stored in a pendant, something the funeral parlour had suggested. I wore the pendant around my neck, but after a while it started to make me feel uncomfortable. As I moved through the day, I would feel it sitting against my chest. It became a constant reminder that he wasn't around anymore. And that's what I missed so acutely, his physical form. I missed seeing him enter a room. I missed seeing *him*. I had to stop wearing the pendant. Then I realised what was happening. Removing his things and taking off the pendant were gestures of release and letting go. But what I really needed was to say goodbye – the final goodbye I didn't have the chance to say.

I sit on the bench where we had our first face-to-face conversation. I'm holding the pendant and thinking back to that conversation, and to the way we were slowly revealing ourselves, beginning to assess each other and trying to decide whether we wanted to see each other again or not. We were noticing things about each other, things that we liked and things that maybe we didn't. I noticed his hands, his beautiful hands, and I remember the way he ran them through my hair after he'd told me could cut hair, that he'd cut previous girlfriends' hair. I noticed his long legs and he noticed my jeans; he told me that he liked them. I remember sitting here, on this bench overlooking the creek, and feeling completely at ease. And that's where I say my goodbye.

I get up and drop the pendant into the moving water. I stand there watching as the water carries it away. I whisper his name and say goodbye and I softly recite a verse from a poem by E. E. Cummings, *I Carry Your Heart With Me*.

'I carry your heart with me, Jev,' I say.

Letting go doesn't mean forgetting. I take my car keys from my pocket and carve his name into the bench. No tombstone, no memorial plaque, just his name on a bench.

Staying in the present, that's become my goal. Instead of wearing the pendant with his ashes around my neck, I now wear a rubber band around my wrist. Every time I notice a thought taking me back to the past, back to sad thoughts, I pull the rubber band and let it snap against my skin. The sudden pain helps bring me back to the present, and helps change the neural pathways in my brain. But I've discovered that it's not an easy thing to do, to change the way we think. I find myself pulling at the rubber band almost all the time. The only time I don't need to do it is when I'm at the parklands. Being there, walking there, helps me be in the *now*. There's no looking back and no looking forward, I'm in nature and in the moment.

I can sense a change in me. I'm not sure exactly what it is, but I've stopped thinking about having lost something. And there's no word to define that loss; we weren't married, I'm not a widow. And I don't have a ring on my finger that I have to take off. We were together for almost three years, but the last year was a difficult one, one dominated by his deteriorating condition. And it's almost a year already since he died. And one day it will be two years and then three, and then he will have been gone for more time that we had been together. Does it matter if it was three years or thirty years that we were together? I'm not sure. I think of the Greek couple married for over fifty years. Yes, maybe it does matter. Maybe it is harder to let someone go after such a long time together. Maybe the sense of loss is greater.

Being older, Jev and I didn't have the possibility of thirty years together. And then his illness was an interruption, as was his death. How would things have gone without that happening? Would we have made it beyond three years? Would we still be together now? I've asked myself those questions many times. I recently read something that stopped me in my tracks: 'Sometimes what you didn't get is exactly what you didn't need.'

I'm not sure how to interpret that, not sure if that could apply to my circumstances. But if it could, the message would be what Maggie Smith writes about in her book: 'Keep moving, no matter what.'

Lately, I've been thinking about my conversation with Julie, about the difference between being alone and lonely. I have had times when I've felt alone, but I don't think I've ever felt lonely. I was married for over twenty years, and there were times in my marriage when I felt very alone. But I haven't experienced living alone. I met Jev only three months after having moved into my new home and, even though we weren't living together, he stayed over regularly. I wasn't completely alone. But it's been almost a year now that I have lived on my own, and I've felt alone. Immediately after Jev's death, I sensed his absence all the time. I waited for his car to come up the driveway. I still checked my phone expecting a message from him. I looked up expecting to see him walk into the room. I started each day in silence, and ended each night in silence too. I suddenly became aware of living alone. But I wasn't lonely; grief and sadness were there to keep me company.

Now that I am ready to move on, now that I'm leaving those things behind, there's a space to be filled. But what *could* fill that space?

I began to experience moments of joy, and not just at the parklands. This morning, when I was on my way to Terra Madre to do my weekly shop, I saw Les walking along Clarke Street. He's an Italian man in his early-eighties who I used to run into all the time when I lived in the area. He is such a dynamic person; he volunteers at St Vincent's Hospital, and I used to see him waiting at the tram stop with his satchel and his walking stick. It had been a while since I'd seen him and I had to stop.

I park in the one spot available and I jump out of the car. As soon as he sees me running across the road, his face lights up, as it always does. He has the most beautiful smile, and I didn't realise how much I'd missed seeing it, and him. We are both overjoyed to be seeing each other again. I speak to him in Italian, and I tell him that I've missed him. I tell him that seeing him always brightens my day. He speaks about otherworldly forces, a guardian angel, that bring us together, and he's so happy that they do. He speaks so kindly, so lovingly, nourishing words of love.

'I love you,' he says, emphasising each word and smiling.

'And I love you, Les.'

He loves me and I love him. I think of him as a positive force, a good force in my life. My dear friend, Les.

Chapter 30

I've recently asked myself what I had to learn from all that's happened. Where is the growth for me? I realise that I've always struggled with change, and possibly without even being aware of it, I've tried to avoid it – as was the case for a long time in my marriage. I stayed married, stayed in a relationship that had run its course, without knowing that was what I was doing. I didn't consciously decide to avoid changing my circumstances to avoid upheaval and discomfort; I simply wasn't aware. It's almost as if I forgot what being happy was. I lost my sense of self. As I said earlier, I was asleep in my life.

But since change had been thrust upon me, it wasn't a matter of choice. Jev was dead. Our life together was over. I was alone. And that was my challenge, to accept and adapt to the changed circumstances, to the pain, to the loss. I left my marriage without looking back, but that wasn't sudden or shocking; I was prepared for it. I've since learned that it's not always that way, and that sometimes we can never be prepared. Things will happen, awful things, and there's no control over that. It's how we choose to respond that we do have control over.

There's a quote that's been attributed to Buddha and the Dalai Lama – the source is unclear – but the message isn't: 'Pain is inevitable. Suffering is optional.' I seriously considered getting that tattooed on my arm. But knowing that, having experienced it, has in some ways been a gift. The gift of change. Even though the road it has taken me on is unknown territory, it's filled with new opportunities. And I'm now better prepared to move towards that new life, more than ever before.

When Robyn Davidson trekked across the desert, she had to learn to live in solitude. She went for weeks without seeing anyone, and found the experience transformed the way she looked at life. Through solitude she discovered an inner world, one that sustained her during her journey. Her experience of living in isolation wasn't a journey of self-discovery, it was *more*. It was an opportunity to question social customs and to find a more authentic way to live. The experience affected the rest of her life and, as she puts it, loneliness can be 'very fruitful.' It's the way she continues to live.

The psychiatrist Anthony Storr wrote a book about solitude. Like Davidson, he talks about the benefits of solitude, and doesn't think the only way to achieve happiness and well-being is through interpersonal relationships. He says they are not the answer to all of our distress, and that solitude can be therapeutic. He acknowledges that love and friendship are both an important part of life and they can bring happiness, but they are not the only way to feel this. And as we get older, they become less important. He suggests that perhaps Nature intended it this way so that the inevitable bereavement that comes with old age causes less distress. Solitude serves a purpose, in particular in times of loss. And coming to terms with loss is something best done alone.

That's not something we hear often. I was conscious of being alone after Jev's death, and more so because of the emphasis that's placed on the importance of *not* being alone. To be alone is often viewed as something not quite right. And even something that evokes pity. Being alone is often equated with being lonely. I discover more and more that isn't the case.

I've always been drawn to solitude. As a young girl I always enjoyed retreating to my room with a book, and spending entire weekends locked away reading. I've always thought that reading the Brontës and D. H. Lawrence at such a young age might not have been ideal. I was drawn to the characters; I understood their predicaments in a way that made me think I had very little in common with other teenagers, male and female. And even though my overly-controlling mother wouldn't allow me to attend social functions with school friends, the truth was that I really didn't want to. I wasn't in search of a boyfriend. The school formal organised with the local Catholic boys school didn't appeal to me, at all. I'd already attended the compulsory ballroom dancing classes at school, where all the girls lined up on side of the hall and the boys on the other; the girls waiting to be asked to dance by the boys. It wasn't the best way to bring awkward teenagers together –

the girls outnumbered the boys and there were always a few girls left standing, trying not to look embarrassed. I would have much preferred to sit in the library until it was all over, and I sometimes did. But I was younger then and worried less – but I wasn't happy.

I think that's the thing about ageing that appeals to me; getting older, we become happier. It's what one researcher describes as the 'paradox of ageing.' And as Storr found, social connections seem to matter less as we age. One study revealed that residents of a nursing home who were happiest and psychologically doing well were those with the least interaction with other people. It really is paradoxical; being alone, they were happier.

I think about the woman I often see standing at the bus stop when I'm driving to work. She's an older woman and always alone, and she's always holding a book open and reading while the noisy traffic whizzes past. She stands slightly stooped, with her head bent and glasses perched on the end of her nose, completely absorbed in her reading. She doesn't look up to watch for the bus and she doesn't seem bothered by the traffic. She's not in a hurry to get anywhere, she's not impatient. She stands immobile, oblivious to what's going on around her. She's waiting for the bus, but if it's late it doesn't matter; it will eventually come. I want to be that woman. Whatever her life has been, whatever sadness or loss or pain she's experienced, she seems far removed from that time. All that has happened is safely in the past. No matter how much life has tossed her about, she now stands serene, untroubled, while the commotion moves around her, not inside her. I want to be that woman.

Getting to work after seeing the woman at the bus stop, I notice the different energy. Walking past the lockers, I'm immediately surrounded by a rush of teenage girls calling out to each other, hugging each other, laughing loudly, and moving very quickly. The energy is frenetic, and I sometimes feel a little overwhelmed as I weave my way through the pulsating noise. And then I think about the woman at the bus stop. *I want to be that woman.*

I've noticed it more and more, the way older people walk at a pace, talk at a pace, live at a pace that isn't hurried or anxious. I watch them closely; I search their expressions, their demeanour. They emanate a calm and an equilibrium that the young don't know. Yes, the infirmities of age can slow people down, but it's more than that. It's a knowingness that *nothing* matters. There is nothing to be rushing towards that matters, that is.

Maybe there is an upside to ageing. And maybe the realisation that the character Philip comes to in the Somerset Maugham novel *Of Human Bondage* is really quite a liberating one. That 'life was insignificant and death without consequence. If life was meaningless then nothing mattered. With that realisation he felt a weight lifted from his shoulders. "Oh, life," he cried in his heart, "Oh life, where is thy sting?"'

Yes, the less importance we give to things, the less they matter.

But I'm not sure I'm quite ready to withdraw from the world into a life of solitude, and I'm not ready for a nursing home either. What I want to do is see where all this is taking me. I want to see where the journey I've been on these past three years leads. The moments of sadness are getting further and further apart, and I'm moving on. I'm being drawn back to life. It's been a challenging journey, and I'm conscious of wanting to erase memories, of not wanting to remember painful events. But memories can't be erased – not until the dementia that old age can sometimes bring does so. And it's not about forgetting. It's about being able to sit with the discomfort of painful memories and letting them pass.

On my way home from the parklands I stop at the lights. I notice a man walking nearby. There is something about the way he moves with long, slow strides, the way his jeans fit him perfectly, and the way his long legs seem to glide along the footpath that catches my attention. Why? Because he reminds me of Jev, the relaxed and laid-back Jev, the way he used to walk. I can't stop looking. I watch as he crosses the road in front of me. His tight-fitting T-shirt accentuating his taught muscles and trim torso. I notice the grey beard and his short-cropped hair. He is an older man but with the body and agility of a much younger man, also like Jev. I can't take my gaze away; I don't want to lose sight of him. And I don't notice the lights change; it's a car horn tooting behind me that reminds me to move on. I have to keep moving.

I've read about people who move on very quickly after the death of a spouse. One man saying that even though he had loved his wife and felt the pain of her loss deeply, the reality was that she wasn't *there* anymore. That was the only thing that was missing, that was the thing that had changed. Apart from becoming acquainted with grief, nothing else was different. He was the same person. And after only a few months, he was able to move on. That's what Hugo Weaving's character in *Love Me* does; he accepts the loss of his wife and moves on very quickly. It turns out that most bereaved people do. They don't get consumed by their grief, and they don't stay stuck in it. They show resilience.

Can I do that? Forget and move on? I am ready to give it a try.

I now know there isn't a right time or a wrong time to start living again. 'There is no 'too soon', as Maggie Smith says. It's always 'on time.' If an opportunity for joy presents itself, it has to be explored. To turn away from it would be like turning away from life. I know I can't do that.

I find myself thinking about *RSVP* Mark. We became friends on Facebook after we met, and I occasionally see his posts. He's still living in NSW and his posts are usually photos of nature and wildlife, and some political commentary – one thing we didn't have in common. But a love of books, yes. In the short time that we saw each other, we discovered a mutual admiration for Anne Tyler. His basic information tells me that he's interested in women and he lists his relationship status as single. So, he's available. I could take up his offer, made before I met Jev, and visit him in NSW. I could do that.

I write a message.

> [I] Hi Mark, do you remember me? Do you remember us? Like two characters from an Anne Tyler novel, I think that's what you said. I was just wondering if you'd like to revisit that novel. I always thought it could be a page-turner. I've been thinking about you, and I've been thinking about how Anne Tyler would write our story. Maybe a different ending?

Do I hit send? I'm not sure. Just as I'm thinking about Mark, I'm also thinking about the man I saw at the parklands a few days ago. It was early in the morning and the sun was shining after a week of grey, dreary weather. Our paths crossed for a few moments; we were walking towards each other and I noticed him looking at me. It wasn't a brief glance and then look away – he kept looking, and he was smiling, a warm, lingering smile. As we drew closer, we said hello and his smile still lingered; the creases on either side of his mouth, a sign of a life filled with laughter. He looked happy.

'Finally, some sunshine,' he said, turning his head as we passed each other.

'Yes, it's a beautiful morning, and so still.'

'Perfect walking weather, even without a dog.'

I laughed.

'Enjoy your walk, and the day.' He seemed to not want to turn away.

'Thank you, and you too,' I said.

He had an energy that made me stop and look back as he continued along the path. Then I had an Elizabeth Strout moment. I once read about her first meeting with her second husband where he turned up at one of her book signings. After she signed his copy of her book, they chatted briefly and then he left. She turned and watched him go, thinking, *That should have been my life.*

I had one of those moments that morning. But unlike Elizabeth Strout's encounter, he hadn't slipped me his email address; she didn't realise that until later. They then started writing to each other and, after meeting twice, moved in together. Another chance meeting, like the paraglider. And Kathy Lette. She also met her new partner later in life, and quite by chance. She was walking in the park and he was sitting under a tree playing Bach on his guitar. She stopped to listen and then they started talking. They exchanged numbers and now they're living together.

Then I remember the message from Jev through the medium: 'Forget me. I'm not worth stopping your life for the rest of your life. Time is precious, remember that.'

As blunt as that message is, and whether it really came from Jev or not, it's nothing more than the simple truth. When death comes – and it always comes – it's final. There's no going back. And we can't stop living; nothing is worth that. Yes, time is precious, life is precious. And I want to feel again the thrill of being alive – whatever that involves: pain, heartbreak, loss, joy.

I think about the man at the parklands. I think about those few moments of connection. I think about his smile. I think about seeing him again. Maybe our paths will cross again.

Maybe.

Acknowledgements

Thank you to all the team at Busybird Publishing for holding my hand through the publishing journey. In particular, I'd like to thank Laura McCluskey for her generous support through the editing process. It was an absolute pleasure working with you.

I'd also like to thank my early readers – Simon Pockley, Rosanna Morales, and Liz Kemp – for their encouragement. And thank you to the team at the Austin Hospital Liver Transplant Unit for their support and care. It really was like being part of a family.

www.ingramcontent.com/pod-product-compliance
Lightning Source LLC
Chambersburg PA
CBHW030257100526
44590CB00012B/427